T0114201

# What the Health?

## By Teenagers, For Teenagers

### Edited By Ms. Sandra Joy Mangarella

Order this book online at www.trafford.com
or email orders@trafford.com

Most Trafford titles are also available at major online book retailers.

Printed in Victoria, BC, Canada.

ISBN: 978-1-4251-3802-8 (Soft)
ISBN: 978-1-4251-6889-6 (e-book)

*We at Trafford believe that it is the responsibility of us all, as both individuals
and corporations, to make choices that are environmentally and socially sound.
You, in turn, are supporting this responsible conduct each time you purchase a
Trafford book, or make use of our publishing services. To find out how you are
helping, please visit www.trafford.com/responsiblepublishing.html*

*Our mission is to efficiently provide the world's finest, most comprehensive
book publishing service, enabling every author to experience success.
To find out how to publish your book, your way, and have it available
worldwide, visit us online at www.trafford.com*

*Trafford rev. 03/24/2010*

 www.trafford.com

North America & international
toll-free: 1 888 232 4444 (USA & Canada)
phone: 250 383 6864 ♦ fax: 812 355 4082 ♦ email: info@trafford.com

We dedicate this book to our friends, families, and all teenagers out there who sometimes feel lost in this crazy life we call adolescence.

# Table of Contents

1. I Know...Who Cares About Nutrition?

2. Isn't It True? Isn't It!? Yes or No!?

3. What Are Growing Pains?

4. Why Me?

5. What Exactly Is Mental Health?

6. Astrological Sign or Life Threatening Situation?

7. What Should I Eat?

8. I Don't Get Enough Sleep... So What?

9. Exercise: What's the Point?

10. What Is An Athlete's Diet?

11. Watch Out For the *Big Girls*?!

12. What's the Skinny?

13. Relationships: Isn't It Funny the Way Things Work Out?

14. So, Did You Guys Do It Yet?

15. Are You Tryin' To Get High?

16. Are You Confident?

# Introduction

What the Health?" started off as an assignment given by our English teacher. What started off as more work to do for school, turned into a mission where WE were assigned to write a book for teenagers by teenagers. What you are about to read discusses the issues that are easy to discuss, and some that are almost taboo.

"What the Health?" is not only an informative and educational book for those that want to read our work of art, but a deeper look at what people think or assume to be true. You will find almost everything about teenage diet and health in this book. Our stories vary from the humorous to the very serious; it's almost improbable that you would find a book about foster kids and masturbating in the same book. Our chapters are very real in their subject matter, and we warn you that we do cross many boundaries in what we write about.

"What the Health?" wasn't written in a way to "beat around the bush." We give you straightforward answers to straightforward questions. We have dedicated our time and effort into giving you, our handsome, wonderful audience, a book in which we shared what we have learned and what we have experienced Our book covers all the basics, from exercise to eating right, and even beyond to drugs and abusive relationships.

We hope that "What the Health?" answers all your questions about being a healthy teenager, and maybe even sparks a feeling of nostalgia to those adults that have gone through all of this already or maybe those young ones that need to know what to expect when they're expecting. . . puberty. In any case, and without further adieu, we now present to you the pouring out of our souls in: "What the Health?"

Ms. Mangarella's AP English Class
-J. Samson

# Forward

"We first make our habits, and then our habits make us."

-John Dryden

What started out as an idea for a book on teen diet and health, ended up to be a very frank yet practical guide on how to survive the teenage years, created by my second period Advanced Placement class. It is not just a book for struggling adolescents who need to develop good mental and physical health habits to get through what can only be termed as very stressful years, it is also a book for parents and teachers to understand exactly what these kids face when growing up. To be honest, I was a bit shocked at how truthful the students were about such things as dealing with mental health, sexuality and the availability of drugs.

My students are athletes, scholars and overachievers in every way, shape and form. They don't get enough sleep, don't eat right and worry about so many things, from getting along with others to getting into college. They were even surprised themselves when they did the research for the book and found that chocolate doesn't really cause acne! They still believed in many things that I believed in when I was their age. They learned to separate facts from myths.

This book is not just a simple how-to guide written by some psychologist or other noted celebrity figure. It is a simple book for teens written by teens. I hope their experiences guide you in making good choices for yourselves.

Thank you very much for supporting their first literary effort. We wish you good health and happiness during your teenage years and for the rest of your lives.

Sandy Mangarella
January 2008

# 1

# I Know... Who Cares About Nutrition?

"As a teenager, nutrition is the farthest thing from your mind right now. You're more concerned with your next date, what clothes you're going to wear to school, and...eww where did that gross pimple come from?"

2

As a teenager, nutrition is the farthest thing from your mind right now. You're more concerned with your next date, what clothes you're going to wear to school, and...eww where did that gross pimple come from? I know what you're thinking- what's the point of caring about nutrition now? I've got my whole life ahead of me- when I turn 30, *then* I'll worry about my health. As teenagers, we all feel invincible. Let's face it; how many teenagers do you know that are diagnosed with acid reflux disease or high cholesterol? Probably not that many if at all. But here's the thing- while *you* may not know many people with these problems, it is not uncommon for teens to experience them. In fact, health problems among teens are a rising issue that society, especially in America, must face.

When we were little kids, our mommies and daddies always told us to eat our veggies because they were good for us. Didn't buy it, did you? Or how 'bout when we weren't allowed to eat too much candy and sugar? I know...it was a bummer. But our parents, as in most cases, had something going for us. Besides the fact that they enjoyed seeing us suffer (just kidding!), they were trying to instill in us the importance of taking care of our bodies. Our bodies are our own personal temples. You can sort of think of it as hmm...ladies, have you ever bought a new pair of shoes or an outfit that you spent your whole allowance or paycheck on? Did you vow to keep them as nice and new as possible? And Guys, have you ever bought a new video game that you spent all your savings on (Yup, I'm talkin' about Halo 3)? Have you ever found yourself saying, "If he gets one single scratch on my game, I'll hurt him"? If yes, then you have the potential to be just as protective to your body. The point is our bodies are waaay too important to ignore. Why? I'm glad you asked. Our bodies are more interesting than you think. Ladies and gentleman, this time in our lives is the most important time to take good care of bodies. I'm going to say that again. LADIES AND GENTLEMEN, this time in our lives is the most important time to take good care of our bodies. Got that? Good. Teenagers need extra nutrients to support adolescent growth.

I Know...Who Cares About Nutrition?

Let me give you a scenario. Jimmy stares at himself in the mirror almost everyday. (Already found something in common? Keep reading). He can't figure out why he has no muscles. He's sixteen and wants to excel on the football team. He considers taking steroids, but he remembers that movie he saw in health class. He can't figure out what to do and decides to take supplements. After all, they aren't dangerous like steroids are- right? WRONG! Fellas, supplements are DANGEROUS. If a girl who knows you take supplements is reading this, you are definitely going to stop soon. Wanna know what they do to you? You'll have to find out later, because I need to talk to the ladies right now.

Ok...so you're in history class and you're suffering. Not only is your teacher boring, but you wanna scream, kick, pull your hair out, anything to make this go away. Yup, you guessed it. It's that time of the month, and you have killer cramps. Tylenol didn't work. Neither did Midol. There's no hope for you; it's just one of those things that you have to deal with in life. Mmm...not quite. I bet you didn't know this, but that saying "an apple a day, keeps the doctor away" has some truth to it. If you like granny smith apples, you're gonna love this. Eating an apple before your menstrual cramps begin and eating it during your cycle will reduce cramps. Does it seem too easy? Exactly. It *is* that easy. It's just a matter of becoming aware of your body's needs and proper nutrition. To both guys and girls, those aren't the only things nutrition is good for. We have A LOT more to go. But for now, let's take it step by step.

Let's start off with breakfast. I know what you're thinking, "Yeah right, like I have time for breakfast." But hear me out. Research shows that eating breakfast not only gives you energy for the day, but it keeps you more emotionally stable. If anyone has ever called you a grouch in the morning, believe them, especially if you don't eat in the morning. Think about it. The last meal you probably had was sixteen hours ago. Sixteen hours ago! You're hungry, whether you realize it or not. Those of you reading this might think to yourself, "I'm in the clear. I eat a doughnut and drink a soda every morning."

Arielle Cannon

**4**

While it is at least something, it might as well be nothing. These types of "meals" only provide you with energy for about a half an hour. After that, your stomach is crying for more, literally. And don't even mention having Physics, Calculus, and Latin Class in the morning. You're doing yourself more harm by not eating. The more difficult your classes, the more you need to make sure that you eat. If you don't know where to start, don't worry.

For starters, you can try blending together a tasty smoothie or shake. You can try blending milk, vanilla, and virtually any fruit in your smoothie. Bonkers over bananas? Add bananas. Crazy about cherries? Throw in some cherries. You can tickle your fancy on this one. If you like cereal, either dry or hot, top it off with your favorite fruit or nuts. I've mentioned these alternatives, but right now you might be thinking, "I'll just stop by McDonald's before school and buy a parfait." Why bother? You can make your own, healthier version at home. Just take some yogurt, fruit, and granola and put it in a glass. You can even customize your own parfait to your liking. McDonald's can't do *that,* can they?

Now Lunch: Your favorite part of the day? Is it because you gorge yourself with juicy, fat, succulent burgers and crispy, salty French fries? While this sounds absolutely delightful, it is only delightful to your taste buds and your stomach for a little while. It may sound dorky, but eating a simple apple and orange at lunch is one of the best things you can do for your body. Try eating a fruit cocktail, applesauce, or even mandarin oranges for a change. You might not realize it, but each day you are eating fatty foods, your arteries are getting clogged more and more. If you don't know what clogged arteries look like, take a look on the internet.

After school snacks anyone? I know, I know. Even more dorkier than what I've been saying before. But don't take your after schools snacks with a grain of salt. (Nice pun, right?) Anyway, eating after school is yet another important thing that so many teens neglect to do. We're so busy with our jobs or hanging with friends or schoolwork that we never take the time to just sit down and treat our bodies the way they are supposed to be treated. Most of the time when you get out of school, you're in need of a quick energy boost. It doesn't even take that much out of your time, so relax. A simple trail mix will do. A great mixture is nuts, sunflower seeds, raisins, and pretzel sticks...the options are limitless. Are you a cheese fan? Can't seem to live without your peanut butter? Use this to your advantage, and use them as spreads on your crackers and fruit. Stomach growling yet? Keep reading...

I probably don't have to remind to eat your dinner. It's most likely the only part of the meal that you actually eat. I'm sure you're thinking to yourself, "Mom's chicken jambalaya or Dad's sloppy joes don't have to call my name twice!" While all of these foods may be extremely yummy and filling, those are not the only types of food out there. Get out there and live! Try new things before you die! The options are limitless, and don't be discouraged from eating healthy foods, too, thinking that you will only be eating tofu burgers and salads for the rest of your life. How does this sound? Chili-rubbed steaks & pan salsa, Mediterranean Portobello burger, oven-barbecued pork chops, poached salmon with creamy piccata sauce...sounds like a part of a menu from an upscale restaurant menu, right? These are just a few dishes that are healthy and take less than forty-five minutes to make. Not only is this healthy and tasty, but Mom and Dad sure won't mind spending half an hour on cooking it either. Are you still disappointed? Are you still thinking to yourself, "Well, that's it for dessert- no more Ben and Jerry's™ ice cream after dinner anymore..." Once again we've got that covered. How do bananas with brown sugar-rum sauce or grilled peaches and angel food cake sound? Get the picture? Let me spell it out for you. JUST BECAUSE YOU EAT HEALTHY, DOES NOT MEAN YOU EAT DISGUSTING, TASTELESS FOODS. That's one thing that is important to learn as a teenager. So many people kill themselves everyday because they have the same false notion and continue eating dangerous foods until they have to undergo triple bypass surgery. Don't let that happen to you.

Arielle Cannon

So, I've already laid out a breakfast, lunch, snack, and dinner menu. Now let's focus on exercise. You may be tempted to flip through the rest of the book at this point, thinking that it does not apply to you. After all you're a teenager; you walk to and from school, and naturally your body is still in good shape. Once again, you may have already convinced yourself that you are going to start an exercise plan by the time you hit thirty. The thing that most people don't realize is that by the time you hit thirty, you may already have health risks that you won't realize until later on. As the saying goes, "Stop while you're ahead." STOP thinking that you are invincible as a teenager. STOP planning for your exercise plans later in life, and just do it NOW. You are at one of the best physical stages right now, so be smart about it, and take advantage. Plus, if your curiosity didn't already lead you to turn the pages, then you'll see why exercise is important when you finally look at it.

First things first. In order to even have energy to exercise, you have to have proper sleep. The average teenager needs nine hours of sleep each night, but only fifteen percent of teenagers get that amount regularly. Most teens get around six hours or less, and even that is considered more than enough for some teens. With all of your schoolwork and extra-curricular activities, how will you ever get the proper amount of rest? It seems like everything is moving so fast. If you don't have a research paper due, you have choir practice. If you don't have a big exam the next day, you have to go to work. The cycle may seem endless, but take it from someone who knows. Mano y mano, teenager to teenager. Don't let things like that keep you from treating your body in the proper way that it needs. I'm not saying to just blow off your schoolwork. But from experience as a work-a-holic, I can truly say that you have to draw the line somewhere. Be smart about it. If you don't get the chance to finish your homework, or you find yourself drooling on your homework assignment at night, do what your body is crying for, and go to sleep. Try your hardest at getting all of your work done, but don't exceed your limits. If you can't finish, try to finish in the morning-do yourself justice, relax, and be honest with yourself. The most logical way you can do to help yourself is to try not to procrastinate. If you still have times when you are overburdened, put the pen down, and give your body what it needs. At an age like this when teenagers and young adults are dying due to stress over schoolwork, society needs all of the living teenagers we can get, including you.

Ok, so now you've got the energy you need to exercise properly. But what kind of exercise can a teen like you really do. At this point in time you most likely don't have the money or the time to spend three hours at the gym. Here's what you can do. Take at least a half an hour to exercise even if it means jogging in place in front of the T.V. or while listening to the radio. As childish as it may sound to some, do jumping jacks and jump rope for a little while. One of the most important things you can do is stretch. Stretching helps the muscles contract and expand easier which means that more blood flow can enter in and out of the heart, which means that your heart won't have to do all the work and will be able to pump blood at a lesser rate. Good activities that develop stamina are running, swimming, and bicycling. A lap or two around the block a couple of days out of the week is just what your body wants. Have common sense too, making sure to never go out alone at night or in the early morning, and don't overexert yourself, thinking that your body can take ten laps around the block without having been trained for it.

Exercise doesn't just benefit your body physically either. Anxiety and chronic fatigue are related to insufficient exercise. Exercising, too, can relieve unresolved stress, which teenagers are notorious for having. Are there students in your school that look like "life sucks for me" all the time? They are most likely depressed or anxious, and with adequate exercise, their frown will turn upside down in a few weeks. Yeah, it's that simple. Would you like to improve your social life? Exercise enhances self-esteem, the ability to learn, raises self-confidence, instills joy in life, and inspires courage to face challenges. Remember when we were discussing sleep and knowing when to draw the

Arielle Cannon

line for homework? Exercising enhances the ability to catch on quicker, so maybe you'll be able to finish your homework quicker, and you'll be able to have those nine hours of sleep you need.

Everything we've talked about this chapter seems like the ideal lifestyle. Healthy food, good sleep, great body...It may seem almost too perfect, like the infomercials you see late at night. But it is real life, and you have the power to decide if it will be your personal real-life story.

Oh yeah, guys, I didn't forget about you. Remember when I mentioned supplements earlier in the chapter? It isn't well known, but supplements have potentially the SAME risks as steroids. Side effects include testicular cancer, infertility (no kids!), stroke, and increased risk of heart disease. If you still don't understand why you should definitely not take supplements think of a girl who knows that you take supplements as reading this, then here's one last picture for you. Supplements can also cause breast development and shrinkage of the testicles. Eeewww!

Arielle Cannon

# 2

# Isn't It True? Isn't It!? Yes or No!?

"We all become very insecure and desperate when puberty hits. We are at the point of vulnerability where we will be too open-minded of how to conquer puberty."

Puberty is probably some of the best years, yet some of the worst years of your entire lives. We're constantly conscious about our physical bodies like how to buff up muscularly, how to shave, how to adjust to these changes, and how to get rid of that demonic acne. Puberty is a science, and I would like to inform you that all you hear on the internet, from friends, peers, and other sources, tends to be false. Just to not complicate things, I won't go into the complex molecular biological stuff when explaining what the facts are and what the myths are. We all become very insecure and desperate when puberty hits. We are at the point of vulnerability where we will be too open-minded of how to conquer puberty. We make these myths the bulk of the information that we put into our brains. Then we make these silly and ridiculous generalizations that chocolate causes our acne to worsen tenfold, shaving too early causes your skin to turn green, shaving frequently makes the hairs so much thicker and darker, or development of hair or other physical features happen overnight. Seems stupid, but can you actually believe some people do take these myths and make them into facts?

It is known that all teenagers are very emotional when puberty makes a first time visit, but with knowledge, comes power. You can either struggle emotionally with your dealings with puberty, or take the measures to dominate puberty and enter into adulthood gracefully. The information will eliminate all these preconceived notions about the typical teenage body under puberty. Believe me, I have undergone the entire process, and I am still constantly battling the acne, the growth changes, and everything else, but I am not nervous anymore because by eliminating the myths and taking in the truth, it will ultimately guide you to a better understanding of this dreaded hellhole called puberty. If you are either a youngster who is very curious about the future or a struggling teenager, this book shows you how you have to watch everything people say about puberty and its dreaded minions. At the end of it, the facts and elimination of myths should guide you but not dominate your entire existence.

Steven Le

# 12
## Acne Myths and Facts

First, let's venture into the world of my number one enemy, acne. Acne has played a terrible role of ruining my skin for many years. There is a lot to blame for acne, but you want to make sure which ones are more accurately to blame.

1. Myth or Fact? Certain foods determine your severity of acne.

It is amazingly a myth. Scientists keep on having studies on this issue, and food has nothing to do with your acne. Acne is the clogging of the skin pores by the build-up of oils. Your chocolate, French fries, deep fried chicken do not cause or worsen acne. Yet, people still believe that foods like pizza, French fries, chocolate, cheeseburgers, and other fatty foods contribute to more acne. If you are still skeptical about it, then eat them sparingly, but sometimes, your mind plays a lot of tricks on you. Your brain has this section called the hypothalamus. It tells your master gland which hormones to produce. Remember puberty is all about your hormones, glands and how your uncontrolled mind can conduct them. Eating French fries and then entirely believing that it will cause acne, can result in acne. This is similar to what psychologists says about a placebo effect, where a person believes he or she is taking a pill but it's sugar, and then they get cured from a condition miraculously; in this acne situation, it would be the opposite. Just be careful; your brain is a very powerful organ, and it can manipulate these things and cause you grief.

2. Myth or Fact? I have to scrub really hard in order to eliminate all the bad stuff that causes acne.

It is another myth! Acne is not something that needs elbow grease (well, that's ironic) in order to eliminate it. Your skin is a very sensitive organ. This myth is one of my downfalls, too; I used to scrub ridiculously hard to exfoliate the dead skin cells, oils, and dust in order to make my skin pores clean and

Isn't It True? Isn't It!? Yes or No!?

clear. That was a detrimental mistake because it did nothing to relieve my skin from the acne. Your skin does not need to be irritated by the damaging scrubbing. Yes, it is actually harmful for your skin but helps the acne because scrubbing too hard can lead to the drying of the skin. This results in your glands producing more oil to moisturize the skin and overdo it to the point where whiteheads, blackheads, and other disgusting pimples began to form again. A light scrubbing is the better way to handle acne. They are alternatives to fighting acne. In fact, moisturizers and other well-known products like Proactive, Oxy scrubs, and Stridex can help fight acne. Fighting acne means cooperating with your skin. Scrub your skin just right with any approved products, such as mild soap and water. That's it. There is no need to go overboard with the scrubbing. Less is truly more when fighting acne.

3. Myth or Fact? Acne is caused by stress.

It is the biggest excuse when I have breakouts, but unfortunately, this is also a myth. Although you have to take into consideration of what I said before, acne is a hormonal issue. You may be flooded with hormones, but people have severe breakouts without stress. Once again, it's our bodies and how differently they function. If you do have anxiety or depression disorders, you may want to look for psychological help, but the only relation to stress and acne is if you are taking medical treatments for that anxiety or depression; as a result, some of their side effects can be a breakout of inflamed unsightly pimples. Regular day-to-day stress is not a factor of acne. If that was the case, 99% of all humans would have breakouts on their faces.

4. Myth or Fact? Acne is primarily caused by oily skin.

This myth may sound the most scientific, but oily skin is a small part of the reason why acne develops. You can dump your head into barrels of oil all day, and acne will not appear, if

Steven Le

14

and only if, there are no bacteria. The biggest culprit of acne is bacteria. Your pores are filled with dead skin cells, oils, and bacteria (if some of you are already unlucky). The bacterium is the one that brews these ingredients to form the plugs or the pus within the pore; as a result, you have your disgusting pimple which may vary from the easily pluck-able whitehead to those unsightly red and inflamed ones. Why do think the word exfoliation appears a lot when it comes to skin care? Exfoliation is the clearing of dead skin cells from the skin's pores. This is very important for everyone, whether you are going through puberty or not. You must remember that acne is at its peak in puberty, but it can stay in your lives for the next ten, twenty, thirty, or forty years! It is vital to have clean pores. By doing so, you are showing everyone healthier and newer skin, and you are definitely eliminating the chance of acne appearing.

5. Acne is not too important for a doctor's appointment.

Acne may be a typical puberty occurrence, but it can appear in many severe forms. When my acne on my shoulders and upper arm became very severe, it was time to visit the dermatologist where she prescribed me a few lotions, ointments, and this special soap called Panoxyl. If you typed in "severe acne" on Google or any other search engine, you can see pictures of the worst forms, where the strongest of antibiotics and lotions would probably be used for that treatment. The most important thing for acne is control, and if you cannot control your outbreaks, then a call for the dermatologist would be needed. Acne is a part of your lifestyle, and its severity will depend on how you will take care of it; therefore, another myth is that you would let acne take its toll, and it would disappear.

<u>Shaving</u>
This part is not only for the guys for the girls as well. We all have to shave sometimes, whether it would be the face for

Isn't It True? Isn't It!? Yes or No!?

guys or the legs for girls. There has been this huge issue whether or not shaving constantly will result in faster growth of thicker and darker hair.

6. Myth or Fact? Shaving a lot will result in thicker and darker hair and will speed up the hair growing process.

This one is a big myth. How can cutting a hair make it grow faster? It's all about genetics. If you are genetically favored to have a ton of hair on your head, face, arms, armpits, and legs, then that is what will happen. Hair growth is controlled by heredity. Shaving is not the only method of hair treatment. There are waxes, which hurt, and you have the tweezers to pluck out the hair. Waxing and tweezing remove the hair as shaving cuts the hair. That explains the stubble and the appearance of dark hair when you are shaving. Another explanation is that more than one hair strand is growing per pore. If you hate the aftermaths of shaving, then explore other methods, like waxing or plucking. You may see a drastic difference.

7. Myth or Fact? Shaving can cause your skin to turn green.

Okay, what idiot made up this piece of information? This is obviously a myth. If your face or skin is becoming green, you should get that checked by a doctor for any diseases like gangrene, where your body or body parts literally rot away, giving a green to black color; gangrene can result in death. You really have to have that shaver put in the most unsanitary conditions in order to get the bacteria to cause gangrene on the face. As a result, simple sanitary shaving will not cause your face or skin to turn green. Shaving is simply cutting hair with shaving creams and such. If you do have an allergic reaction to a shaving cream or substance, then you should be very cautious when buying and using a product. Green as a humanly color most likely represents rotting and decaying

Steven Le

16

of the skin and body parts. The simple routine of cutting facial hair has no chemical properties to turn the face green.

<u>Body Odor</u>

What really is body odor?  Could it be that stench that is sweat?  Most teenagers have problems with body odor, and we rely on deodorants, antiperspirants, and body sprays like Axe™ to repress the noticeable body odor.  For those who use deodorants and antiperspirants, you are doing the right thing because body odor thrives on sweat, but can it be the culprit?

8. Myth or Fact? Sweat is smelly, and it is the source of body odor.

Sweat is actually is not smelly at all because it is actually odorless.  Sweat is a diluted form of urine where it is composed mostly of water with sodium and other electrolytes (a fancy term for ions of different elements).  The odor is the job of bacteria; somehow, these terrible creatures get into areas like under your armpits, hair, feet, and upper thigh region.  This is why most athletes take showers after their practice or game because they are clearing all the bacteria from their body; as a result, there is no body odor.  All you can really do is just keep on using those products and take showers frequently. It does not hurt to use those body sprays as extra insurance if body odor develops during school or work.

9. Myth or Fact? Diet is a factor when it comes to body odor.

Finally, we have a fact. There are other factors for body odor, and diet and nutrition is one of them.  Have you ever heard that some smells develop from a certain kind of food like garlic, curry, or fish?  Well, what you smell is probably what was eaten.  Studies have proven that your diet affects how concentrated your sweat is.  The more concentration of molecules and electrolytes is like an all-you-can eat buffet for

Isn't It True? Isn't It!? Yes or No!?

bacteria; the bacteria multiply exponentially, and their wastes would result in the gaseous body odor that we all despise.

10. Myth or Fact? Genetics is a factor when it comes to body odor.

This is also a fact. For genetics, body odor links itself to the immune system and a system of molecules called major histocompatibility complex. The amount produced is determined by your genes, and the variations of genes means there are people with different concentrations of these molecules.

Nutrition

Our bodies are developing, and we need to be very cautious of what we put into them as certain foods and substances can affect the outcome at adulthood. Nutrition is a part where you develop a lifestyle of how you eat. A lot of people have a high metabolism or low metabolism; metabolism is the process where your body uses these digested foods and converts them into the energy that the body can use effectively. This section is critical to realize how certain foods are underestimated or overestimated with its nutritional content. At the end, it is about balance. Balance is the key to maintaining a good diet and a good life.

11. Myth or Fact? Fat-free is calorie free.

Every single thing inedible or edible in this universe contains energy. You have to realize that a calorie is a unit dealing with the amount of energy in a food product. If there is no energy, there is no substance. If you have the same amounts of fat, sugars, protein, the fat will obviously have more calories. Sugars and proteins do contain calories, too. A couple of slices of bread is equivalent to a tablespoon of olive oil calorie-wise. Because it lacks fat, it does not mean you can eat so much more. You may be harming yourself further because these fat-free foods can only go so far. An excess of the fat free foods may as well be as bad as the fatty foods because of the calories. The key to this idea is to look at your nutrition labels and look at the serving size. As a result, you can indulge on those fat-free foods without binging, eating at a higher capacity in one sitting.

**12.** Myth or Fact? Eating an irregular amount of salt will kill you.

This may still be debated, but this is a myth, as salt is a mandatory mineral that you must consume in order to live. Your nervous system is composed of tissues, which are composed of cells called neurons. These neurons need the sodium in salt in order to function really well. If you consume a lot of salt, you want to eat a good portion of potassium to balance the content. An excess of salt may cause high blood pressure, but it is a minor contribution. High blood pressure and arterial problems are most likely caused by the clogging of saturated fats and/or your own genes. Salt dissolves in water, and it cannot clog up your arteries or veins. You need salt to live because you cannot function at all if you have a sodium and potassium deficiency.

Eat all the salt you can, but eat a good amount of potassium to prevent any minor health issues. Avocados, potatoes, bananas, broccoli, orange juice, soybeans and apricots are the best sources for potassium, but each of them varies in their concentrations of potassium. Studies have proven that a diet high on potassium can reduce hypertension, another term for high blood pressure. Salt cannot really kill you by consuming irregular amounts. Once again, it comes to the fact that everyone has different bodies due to our genetic makeup. If you do not have a family history of high blood pressure, then salt is not your enemy.

If you do have a family history of it, then you may want to watch your salt intake. It has very minor health effects, but it is a necessity of life.

## 13. Myth or Fact? Vegetarian diets are so much healthier.

The word vegetarian has its loopholes; as a result, the word associates itself with health, skinny, and longevity. Obviously, a vegetarian diet consists of non-meat products. A person who begins a vegetarian diet may result in deficiencies that proteins from meats can fulfill. A vegetarian must get all the vitamins and minerals from different sources. Protein is a required thing that all humans must consume in order to live. If there is no protein, our bodies can begin to shut down because these proteins are used to make nearly everything in our bodies. Soybeans are a great source of non-meat protein.

A person can easily become unhealthy by living on the constant consumption of French fries, grilled cheese sandwiches, nuts, and many non-meat products. Although nuts do take care of a few vitamin deficiencies, five to six handfuls can easily be equivalent to of eating a few tablespoons of fat. Nuts also vary in their oil abundance. People who snack on the fattier nuts need to take the same precautions as those who eat junk food; too much of a good thing is a bad thing. In a study, nut eaters tend to live two to three years more than non-nut eaters because they tended not to snack on junk food.

As a result, a vegetarian diet does not mean it is a non-fat diet; a lot of these oils and fats still exist in non-meat products. Like the meat-eaters, it is important to watch the intake of these foods. I can conclude that this statement above is a myth.

## 14. Myth or Fact? Eating after 6:00pm, or 7:00pm, or 8:00pm, or any time late at night is bad because the food will turn straight into fat.

Steven Le

The reason why many people state this is because most of our calorie intake is during the morning, midday, and afternoon. Our bodies are not switches where we decide what time is right where we metabolize foods into fats, proteins, and other organic molecules. By nighttime, we have consumed most of our calories; therefore, the further consumption of calories during the night may result in weight gain because weight gain is caused mainly when our calorie intake succeeds the amount that we need to live.

**15. Myth or Fact? Processed foods are not as nutritious as natural foods.**

This is a myth, and at times, processed foods are as or more nutritious than natural foods. Let's take frozen vegetables for an example. These vegetables are harvested at their prime, and they are frozen in their prime; as a result, the quality of the frozen vegetables is as good as the non-frozen ones when they thaw because they retained their nutritional value. You must take into consideration of how vegetables today are transported. The transportation of vegetables may take days; this would result in the natural aging process where the vegetables may spoil, and they would lose a majority of its nutritional value. This is true because most grocery shopping veterans meticulously try to search for the best tomatoes, onions, apples, oranges, and other fresh produce. I remember going shopping where it would be so frustrating to try to pick which fruits and vegetables were fresh enough to cook with. If you go into a farmer's market where the vegetables and fruits are hand-picked on that day, then you would not have to worry about quality and nutritional losses.

Food engineering is a booming industry where engineers try to incorporate as many minerals, nutrients, and fibers into many products like cereals, soups, breads, and many canned foods. There are ingredients that you would need a biochemist to interpret, but some of these ingredients would be a benefit to your health.

Isn't It True? Isn't It!? Yes or No!?

## What can we conclude?

There are a lot of things from our media, peers, families, friends, and other people that may not be true. It is important that you have the ability to determine which things are the truths and which things are the lies. Puberty is a phase in our lives where our body literally goes haywire, but it goes crazy for the betterment of developing ourselves into adults. This is a time where we are gullible and easily influenced by many sources. Some of these myths can sound like reasonable facts where it can be easily manipulated to sway teenage society.

Make sure you look up anything that may sound unusual or doubtful to you. Learning is a part of having an open mind, but it is also when you know which information to accept and which one to reject; skepticism is a part of learning. When we question others, we finally think for ourselves; we become independent from sources that can easily manipulate. Think for yourself. Do not take a piece of information and make it a part of your existence in a blink of an eye. Sometimes, information must be taken like a grain of salt.

These myths and facts should guide you and clarify all the misconceptions of acne, shaving, body odor, and nutrition. Enjoy puberty with knowledge, not gullibility and ignorance.

Steven Le

# 3

# What Are Growing Pains?

"If you accept yourself as who you are, then you will achieve everything you want in life."

Have you ever looked in the mirror and asked yourself, "Is this my body?!" Has it ever been hard for you to button a pair of jeans that had just fit? Did you ever wake up in the morning with a monster growing on your face? Did you ever feel a strange odor was coming from your body and everyone else noticed? Have you ever just been uncomfortable or self conscious with your body? Don't worry, you are not alone. All these changes you are going through are merely just growing pains! Pimples on your skin, growth of hair on weird places, and body odors are all normal! I have experienced them, your friends have experienced them, and you will, too. There is nothing to be embarrassed about. The human body is like a world full of growth and changes.

Your body will grow in all sorts of directions. We are all prepared for physical growths. Girls know that their breasts will grow, and boys expect to become more muscular. Let me make this clear once again; do not be embarrassed! All of this is normal. Girls, your breasts will start to grow, and you will need to become comfortable with that. I remember my first experience with this situation. I thought it was all weird; I did not even feel comfortable going out and buying a bra. But I now realize that all this is normal, and being weird about it is just useless. Now guys, you will experience changes, too. Your voice will start to change, your bodies will experience much growth, and you will start to get facial hair. Guys also tend to sweat a lot more then girls during puberty. This can cause odors! But there is a solution; use deodorant! Girls, make sure you use deodorant also. You may also smell body odors coming from other places, but no one else can notice it. So do not worry. These are just signs of growing up, so no need to get all crazy about it.

Guys and girls will also start to notice growths in unusual places, such as the butt or the belly. Others will grow much taller or much skinnier. Some people grow a temporary layer of fat to get the body ready for a growth spurt. Some people eat healthy foods and still gain weight. However, there

Raahi Upadhyay

are other people who eat a lot and gain no weight. Believe me, I know how this feels. I do not eat much; however, I feel like I gain weight. I have friends who eat much more then me, and they are so skinny. This just has to do with your metabolism. Eventually, everything will balance out, and you will learn how to adjust to your body. Now, let's get in-depth and personal! Let's start with the girls!

Growing up as a girl is both scary and exciting! No one said growing up is easy, but it's not life ending either. Are you tired of having people tell you, "Oh, you are just going through a phase; you'll get over it?" Do you feel as if no one understands how you feel? Everything may seem scary, but puberty is just another challenge on your way up to adulthood. Everything seems to change, but these changes help you learn more about yourself. You probably have so many questions in your brain that you are scared to ask. This is completely normal! I have asked my mom such crazy questions. You are not the only one facing these questions, but the best approach is to ask a woman you are close to. If you feel awkward about this, then I will try my best to answer them in this chapter.

**When do puberty and "growing pains" begin?**

In girls, puberty usually begins sometime between the ages of nine and thirteen. It will last for about three years and usually ends by the time a girl reaches the age of sixteen. There are two signs which initiate the start of puberty: the growth of breasts and the growth of pubic hair. Do not get scared about all these changes! Everything will be okay at the end; it is all part of growing up. Another topic all girls worry about is getting their period. Learning about getting your period is scary. When I first got it, I thought there was something physically wrong with me. But there wasn't. You will always remember the day when you get your first period. It is a very special day in a young girl's life. It is when she starts to make her way into womanhood. Girls tend to get their period between the ages of
nine and sixteen. Getting your period may cause you to ask many questions.

**What Are Growing Pains?**

**What is normal?  How long will I have my period? How often will I get it?  Does it hurt?  Is it ok to use tampons?**

All bodies are different; therefore, answers to these questions vary for all girls.  But there are some similarities. You will usually get your period every 28 days or every 35 to 40 days.  Periods are irregular for the first two or three years.  It is a good idea to keep track of when you get your period on a calendar.  Periods usually last from two to three days to seven days.  It is normal to have it for ten days, only if bleeding is not heavy.  Getting your period may be painful if you do not eat and exercise properly.  These pains are called cramps.  It is good to take a Tylenol™ or Advil™ during your period.  It is absolutely normal to use a tampon.  Some people have a crazy idea that using tampons will cause you to lose your virginity. This is the biggest load of garbage I have ever heard.  Tampons are completely safe from a medical standpoint.  Pads could also be used.  Pads are safer and more comfortable.  Apart from getting your period, you may have other questions about your body.

**Will my breasts get any larger?**

Breasts experience growth in five different stages and are fully developed by the age of 17 or 18.  The sizes of breasts do not determine anything! So, girls, do not get self-conscious.

**How do I get rid of acne?**

Washing your face is an easy approach.  This will remove all the oils on your face, which cause acne.  Also, stop using so much make up and so many different kinds of creams.  These chemicals are bad for your skin and make acne worse.  People think eating chocolate and drinking caffeine can cause acne, but this is just a myth, so eat away! Do not pick your pimples!  This will only cause the acne to spread.  If your acne is horrible, then it would be a good idea to see your dermatologist.  Also, try some over the counter medicines that are made to reduce acne, such as Clearasil™.

Raahi Upadhyay

**Do I need to lose weight?**

"Hey, do you think I look fat?" How many times have you asked or have been asked this question? It is good to be concerned about your weight, but do not obsess about it. It is normal to gain some weight during puberty; however, make sure you do not become overweight. The best thing to do is exercise which keeps your weight balanced throughout your teen years. This is because it will be hard to lose this weight once you become an adult.

**Why are my emotions so crazy?**

Do you feel like you are on an emotional roller coaster? You may get sad and angry over the smallest issues. This is completely normal. The hormones in your body are continuously changing, which affects your emotional behavior. Once puberty is completed, your ride on this emotional roller coaster will end also.

**How do I know when puberty has ended?**

Puberty is basically completed when pubic hair attains an adult pattern. The pubic hair will be in an inverted triangle, covering the entire pubic area, with some extension of hair down the inner thighs. Also, puberty is complete when your breasts are adult configuration.

I hope this in-depth analysis of puberty has helped! If you still have more questions, do not be embarrassed to ask your mom or any other woman in your life. Guys, I have not forgotten about you! Just like girls, guys have questions and concerns about their body too. Girls may think we suffer a lot of growing pains; however, guys are in the same situation.

If you are a normal teenage boy, then you must have questions about what's going on with your body. For some reason, I have noticed that it is so much harder for boys to ask questions dealing with their bodies. You guys must understand that puberty is an exciting part of your life! The first step in understanding puberty and your body is to know that your questions and concerns are completely normal. The next step is to know that you are not the only one with questions, and men of all ages have gone through the same changes you are experiencing now. If you are still uncomfortable with asking someone your questions, I will try my best to answer them here.

**When does puberty begin and what happens?**

The first sign of puberty will be the enlargement of your testicles. This will probably occur during the same time as the appearance of pubic hair. Body odor and facial hair will become noticeable also. Use deodorant! Puberty usually starts to take place between the ages of 10 ½ and 13 and usually lasts until the ages of 17 or 18.

**Why does my voice change?**

Changes in your voice are due to the structural changes in your larynx or voice box. A change in voice usually occurs in early puberty when boys start to produce testosterone. There is then a gradual change or deepening of voice throughout puberty. The age for completion of voice change is between the ages of 14 and 16.

**Is it normal to have lumps under my breasts?**

Gynecomastia is the term that describes the extra tissue or "lumps" around your nipples. This occurs in about 70% of teenage boys. During puberty, the small amount of breast tissue that all men have responds to hormones, such as testosterone and eventually enlarges due to the pressure from clothes. Boys may jump to ridiculous conclusions, such as they are developing breasts, or they have cancer. This is completely incorrect. These lumps last for about a year and then eventually disappear. There are no medications to remove lumps; however, surgery can be done in severe cases. I do not recommend surgery; you should just let nature take its course.

**Can I increase the size of my penis?**

The penis is not a muscle, so "exercising" it will not make it grow. Despite what you have heard, masturbation has no effect on the size of your penis either. Once puberty is complete, your penis has reached its adult size, and nothing will make it grow any further.

Raahi Upadhyay

### Is it normal for boys to have acne?

Yes, it is completely normal for you to have acne, and you are not the only teenager facing this problem. Acne is due to the increased hormone levels which cause the oils that cause acne to develop. Acne will eventually disappear; however, to reduce it, you can buy many over the counter medications. If it is extremely severe, then you should make a visit to your dermatologist.

I hope these questions and answers helped both the girls and the guys. Now experiencing such changes can cause you to have many emotional changes. You may feel like no one understands you; however, you must learn to not let it affect you. You may feel that your parents do not understand, but you should try talking to them. It might help.

Experiencing puberty is extremely exciting; however, it can also cause periods of fluctuating emotions for both girls and boys. These emotions are mostly due to having images of the ideal body. Our media does not help this image but only worsens it. You should never compare yourself with others; you should always be happy with what you have. If you do not like your self-image, then try to change it, but do not act like it is the end of the world. Once again, you are not the only person who is self-conscious about his body. Your self-image can also be influenced by success in sports, school, peers, and how well you meet all these expectations. Believe me; my high school years have been completely ridiculous. Trying to keep up with my school work and understanding my family and friends has been so hectic. Even I have had some doubts about my self-image, but I now realize that you are who you are, and you should be happy with it. If you accept yourself as who you are, then you will achieve everything you want in life. You may also suffer growing pains by having endless arguments with your parents. You and your parents may disagree on various topics; however, keep in mind that they want the best for you. It is important to have love and guidance during this time, so do not overlook it when it comes your way.

### What Are Growing Pains?

Experiencing growing pains causes questions for both girls and boys. This is both an exciting and a confusing time for both. As you girls become women and you boys become men, you will not only learn more things about yourself but will begin to understand yourself on many levels. To achieve this understanding, you must know what is going on with your body. You must ask questions without feeling shy. During this process, you may also have many doubts about yourself, but try not to let this affect you in a negative way. Take all the new changes in a positive manner, and everything will turn out perfectly all right.

Raahi Upadhyay

# 4

# Why Me?

"Start by developing a more stable health care plan that works not only for me but for other children that are in the system and just want to live."

The foster care system is so corrupt that it fails to play a significant role in assisting children that are in the system in the health care and/or diet that they may need. The Division of Youth and Family Services, also known as DYFS, are responsible with providing us foster children with the essential healthcare we need and how ways to can make our life as "normal" as possible.

However, they seem to let us down time and time again when we need and want that support from them, our only source. We are limited to the benefits that we are allowed to receive, and many of us don't speak on it because of fear. These fears are the fear of being rejected and denied, (as our parents and caretakers have done to us), and the fear of not knowing how or when to ask for what we want and need.

From coast-to-coast, it seems to be getting more and more difficult to treat the mentally, emotionally, and physically troubled children in their care. Meaningless doctor visits, psychiatric drugs, and record keeping cover up the real issue of health care for foster children. Being in the foster system causes many issues to arise, and these can be life-altering and can occur at any moment. As foster children we never know what is going to happen to us next, so we wait and see whatever is in store for us; we accept it and move on. Or at least that's how I get along, and if I might say, it has worked very well for me. Not many people seem to think so though.

They say it's not healthy and that I can't survive by keeping my emotions and feelings bottled up inside. I need to release that anger and find peace and contentment in my life. That sounds all well and good, but it's hard trying to pursue that, especially when people see that you are in foster care. They look at you as if you are a disease, or they feel bad because you are less fortunate.

The number of children in foster care is increasing in size, and this causes a setback because that means the government has to provide and give that much more to these children who come in with absolutely nothing. Children enter the foster care system due to experiences that are or

Carnita Tyler

have been detrimental to their health and well-being, which include child abuse and neglect. Great numbers of infants and many young children that have a complicated and serious physical, mental health, and developmental problems are now being placed in foster care. These children in foster care need to receive initial health screenings and assessments of their medical, mental, dental health, and developmental status to make sure they are okay; we don't want to lose any of them.

Other serious reasons why children are placed in foster care are because of neglect that occurs because of the parents' drug or substance abuse, extreme poverty, mental illness, homelessness, or the human immunodeficiency virus (HIV) infection, fear, and not having the education needed to know what it means to take care of a child.

Being in the system, foster children are subject to experiencing the poor end of healthcare. Not receiving the medicine or treatment needed leads to growth and developmental issues and mental health issues. Many different placement transitions occur because of the health issues that foster children have. Many are placed in different centers of care, such as juvenile detention centers, foster homes, shelters, mental health centers, and even in special education. Foster children age out of the foster care system at the age of 18, before they are mentally ready to live on their own.

The health care for these children consist of four different components: initial health service, comprehensive health assessment, the developmental and mental evaluation, and the primary care and monitoring. Each child should have an initial health screening before or shortly after being placed at any foster home or child care facility. There should be an inspection of the body, because many children have been victims of physical and sexual abuse, and any bruises and scars should be noted and brought to someone's attention. Any chronic illness and/ or medication being taken should also be noted.

The comprehensive health assessment should be performed about one month into the foster child's placement to prepare them for the primary ongoing services. All past medical and social family information should be available to any physician that is performing the assessment. Since children that are entering the system come from substance and physical abuse settings, they are considered at high risk for chronic illnesses and sexually transmitted diseases.

With each health visit, the physician should consider and attempt to do a developmental and mental health evaluation. This ensures that the child is socially, emotionally, and mentally healthy. This assessment can be based on interviews or psychological evaluations done by a certified doctor or social worker. The results from the performed assessment should be recommended and incorporated into the child's case.

Last but not least, primary care and the monitoring of the child's health is critical while in foster placement. There are different problems and changes that may occur over time while in placement because the actual move and placement can be stressful for the child. Check ups are important and imperative. Each and every social worker should keep updates on each child's progress. This is the health process that DYFS should have each child go through but it doesn't always work out that way.

Writing this book and being able to be a part of this with my AP English class is a great thing. It brings me out of my box and lets me pour all of my feelings, thoughts, and knowledge of what I know about the system out on paper. I have always wanted to write a book about the foster care system, but it's hard, because you never know what to say or better yet, how to say it. It's like you have it in your head ,and you want to tell someone about it but you can't find the right words to say and you're afraid of what people might think. The chapter of the book about Foster Children's Health Care, really hits close to home. I have been in foster care since I was

Carnita Tyler

four years old. So basically I was born into it, and I have seen the ups and downs, and the ins and outs of the system. Health care has always been an issue because as a child without a mother or father to care for you and take you to all your doctor visits and appointments for your immunization shots, it kind of sucks for us.

I was placed in foster care because my mother was incapable of taking care of me. She would rather spend our grocery money on crack and weed than feed and nurture her children. I tried to convince myself that she just didn't know, but it all boils down to her not caring, and being without her children was better than being with them because of that freedom she obtained. I was healthy with maybe a couple of cavities because of all the chocolate I ate, but I was okay. It's funny how people look at you so differently from society when you are in foster care. They are afraid and don't know how to approach you. It's like if you're in a group of people and someone says something disrespectful about your mother, and you tell them you are in foster care, they get this sudden look on their face, like the world is coming to an end. I laugh because I know they don't mean any harm, and they didn't know.

That goes to show that you should think before you speak, and you never knew what someone situation may be and what they could be going through.

Tell me: What is the first thing that comes to mind when you hear, "I am in the foster care system"? Most people automatically think of the other person's mother or father. They ask you what happened, and want to know where your mother is. At one time in my life when I lived in a shelter, one of the child care worker's daughters asked me if I had a baby. I looked at her and said I was only 16. Not that you can't have a baby at the age of 16, but that's not a question every sixteen year old is asked. It took a minute for me to realize that when people think of you as being in foster care and not having a "family," they began to assume things. There have been many girls and boys that I have known and lived in a shelter with that have had the same opportunities and chances that I have had, and they did not make the right decision.

Many of the girls have gotten pregnant and dropped out of school; the boys may have contracted a STD or have begun to sell drugs and harm society. Each person that I have known for that little amount of time have come to the conclusion to what they want to do with their lives. It all ends with their spiraling downhill, crying out for help.

I didn't have that sense of security and support system that many other children may have with their parents or guardians. At times, I feel like maybe I should be a part of another world, like there should be another community for children that are in the foster care system. It's like I want to isolate myself because I am so different, and I come from a different background and I may not have what others have and know what they know. Then again, we all come from different backgrounds and know and have different things, and it took me a while to realize that because I was so determined to try and fit in a perfect society.

Sad to say, but nothing is perfect.

Being abandoned by your mother is not perfect, being placed in foster care isn't perfect, not knowing who your father is not perfect, being hurt mentally, physically, and emotionally is not perfect, but you learn to cope with it and create something so much better for you. I don't blame the foster care system for what I have experienced and been through. I do, however, expect them to care for them the way they should, and give me what I need in order to live a better healthier life. Many of the people that work within the health care system that tend to children in foster care, don't even like their jobs.

This causes a big problem within the health care system because if there are people that don't care about what they do for a living, they are not going to put their all into helping us. It all goes back to the procedures of what must be done to establish daily check-ups and maintain the health care for the foster child.

Carnita Tyler

36

Being in foster care has taught me a lot. It has taught me to go for whatever I believe in and not let anyone or anything get in the way of my happiness. But most importantly, it has taught me to never depend on anyone but myself. I am all I have, and in a world like this, that's all I may ever have. I thank the people that work the foster care system, and I appreciate their courtesy. I just wish that instead of putting us down as foster children that have no goals, values, or morals and think we will do anything just to get by, they should lift us up and make us into mature, respectful adults.

Start by developing a better more stable health care plan that works for everyone.

Carnita Tyler

# 5

# What Exactly Is Mental Health?

"These are the things we have to struggle with every day, even when no one else sees that something is wrong, and no one seems to care."

What exactly is mental health? Mental health is a person's psychological well-being and adjustment to society and to the ordinary demands of life. So in normal terms, mental health must be something like keeping your cool when the world is crashing down on you. I mean, what exactly are ordinary demands? Are there cases where you're not expected to be mentally stable? What about when you have to complete college applications, and you're up until 4:30 in the morning because you had no other time to do them, and now they're due tomorrow? They're the most important thing because your future depends on those silly papers, but funny enough, you don't have time to care about them. Besides that, you have to write a half-hour speech for your church group that you're going to deliver to 300 strangers, and that's supposed to be your priority. HA! Priorities? That's a funny concept because everyone demands that everything be your top priority. Clearly, that cannot be fulfilled. On top of that, your grandfather passes away, and you're sitting at the funeral with your homework on your mind because you can't even function enough to appreciate the important moments in life. How about when you have five hours of ridiculous homework assignments every single night, because selfish teachers don't understand that the world doesn't revolve around their class? When you have to go home, and somehow manage to write a research paper, 700 essays, and other worthless assignments due within mere days of each other, to the point where you can't even worry about the important things in life, such as the grief of losing a family member - it's not so easy to keep your cool, is it? This is especially vital when you have to do this over and over on 2 hours of sleep. Procrastination is not a factor in this one, because you can work every single moment, and still not be able to keep up with the amount that needs to be done.

Some people can handle things better than others, but when teachers just pile on the work like it's nothing, it can break even the best of us. Kids, these days, are expected to handle a lot of stress, but it gets to a point where it's ridiculous and infuriating. Why doesn't anyone seem to understand that

Celeste Schimmenti

students have many other important things on their mind? My example above is personal, but I can guarantee that many other teenagers also face these kinds of difficulties at one time or another. High school is a stressful environment, especially when no one is considerate of how each individual is handling things. This is why we see school shootings and outbreaks every so often, because students are mentally unstable, and no one even takes the time to pay attention to them. Mental stability is not something that should be taken for granted because in today's fast-paced, stressful environment, it's hard to come by.

Mental stability is being able to handle stress in a positive way, but what's the limit? How much can one person possibly handle before they lose it? Ask an honors student, and the answer may vary from a student who is not forced to work so hard. So who puts all this pressure on us? Teachers? Parents? Ourselves? Nevertheless, it's there. No high school student can succeed, yet avoid stress. Each of us must be able to handle it positively to some extent, and work through it in order to gain the confidence to succeed.

Stress is what pushes us to strive to do better. It's what forces us to function under even the toughest conditions. It heightens our awareness in the world, and in effect, helps us to protect ourselves from danger. Despite its positive and natural aspects, excessive stress can be negative. Some signs of negative stress are:
-Excessive frustration
-Alcohol and drug usage
-Feeling very angry or very worried
-Feeling grief for a long time after a loss or death
-Thinking your mind is out of control
-Hurting other people or destroying property
-Doing reckless things that could harm yourself or others

What are some ways to handle stress? Some advice includes taking deep breaths, relaxing, exercising, eating, and

What Exactly is Mental Health?

avoiding excessive caffeine. A big way to let out stress is to talk about it with others, whether they are parents, older adults, or friends. While this may help, sometimes you just need to get to work and get things done. Nothing is a better stress reliever than accomplishment.

Even in some cases, all of the above fail to relieve stress. This is when we, as teenagers, may turn to negative methods of relief. At times, everything can start to weigh too much, and we all too often make bad decisions to alleviate the way we feel.

One common misconception is that drugs and alcohol will make everything feel better. This is the basis of addiction. When we turn to drugs to mask the effects of our problems, we become dependent on them to make us feel good. The future consequences of drug and alcohol abuse prove to be so negative, yet so many teens become addicted every day. We need to do everything we can to avoid these harmful influences.

Taking care of our bodies when there are just so many other things to worry about is often hard. Some people binge eat, don't eat, or don't exercise. Your body should be one of your top priorities, despite everything else that you need to take care of. Binge eating can be harmful because it can cause excessive weight gain or loss. The body needs a steady supply of nutrients in order to function. The same goes with starvation. You cannot possibly work hard or focus without food in your body. Exercise is often beneficial to health and also as a stress-reliever. Even if you're not used to exercising, even just going for a walk can sometimes be relaxing and soothing.

The teenage brain supposedly needs more sleep than a growing baby's in order to function appropriately. Now how many teenagers actually sleep 12-14 hours a day? I can guarantee the answer to that question is near zero. Decreasing amounts of sleep lead to higher stress levels and higher risks of physical illness. Sleep is an essential part of a healthy everyday routine that many teens take for granted.

Celeste Schimmenti

When all else seems to fail, many teens' mental health suffers. There is a wide range of mental disorders that stem from or cause struggles during the teenage years. One of the most common of these is depression.

Everyone feels depressed at one point or another, especially teens. It truly can't be avoided, especially because we all have raging hormones. Between boyfriend and girlfriend troubles, issues with parents, and fights with friends, all of us will eventually come across a reason to be depressed, and this can affect us greatly. Most of the time, it's easy to "snap out of" within a few days or a few weeks. When someone mentions the word depression, we think of this. Yes, it stinks, but it's part of life.

Depression, medically, on the other hand, is a little different. This is when the common feeling of sadness lasts for a longer period of time and can interfere with life. It is caused by an imbalance of brain chemicals, along with other factors, and like any serious medical condition, depression needs to be treated. This can include therapy and even medication when conditions are extreme. Even the worst cases of depression are treatable, so no one should ever lose hope.

If depression goes untreated, the results can often be devastating and horrifying. When a person is depressed, they usually can't think clearly or with long-term goals in mind, and they often feel that they will be depressed and miserable forever. This is why many teens turn to suicide. It's a common tragedy. Every teen just needs to understand that they're not alone, and that people care about them no matter what the circumstances are. Even the people that seem to care the least, honestly do care in the end. Anyone feeling as though they have no purpose should really seek the help and support that is truly so easy to find.

A main group of mental disorders stem from anxiety disorders. "Anxiety disorder" is a term covering several different forms of abnormal, pathological anxiety, fears, and phobias. These fears are irrational or illogical and not based on fact.

**What Exactly is Mental Health?**

Anxiety is frequently accompanied by physiological symptoms like fatigue and exhaustion. This can sound familiar to all of us. So how do we know if we are just stressed, or have a mental disorder? For example, look at this quiz:

-Do you experience tenseness while at rest?
-Do you have a fear of losing control or going crazy?
-Do you avoid social situations?
-Do you have fears of specific objects?
-Do you fear that you will be in a place or situation from which you cannot escape?
-Do you feel afraid of leaving your home?
-Do you have recurrent thoughts or images that refuse to go away?
-Do you feel compelled to perform certain activities repeatedly?
-Do you persistently relive an upsetting event from the past?
-Do you experience chronic stress?

If you answered yes to more than half, then there's reason to say you should follow up with a visit to a mental health professional for a full evaluation. This is ridiculous. These questions are completely general, and just like "medical school syndrome," you may feel as though because you answered yes to these, you have an anxiety disorder and need help. This is not true, but it does demonstrate how fine the line is between being mentally stable and unstable. Everyone feels these things at one point; it is only once the feelings interfere with everyday life, that there may be a significant problem.

Obsessive-compulsive disorder (OCD) is a psychiatric anxiety disorder most commonly characterized by obsessive, distressing, intrusive thoughts and compulsions. The routine tension and stress that appear throughout life with an anxiety disorder are often present in OCD. Once again, a person may feel like they have this disorder if they know the symptoms:

Celeste Schimmenti

-When thoughts, impulses, or images are excessive worries about unrealistic problems.
-The person attempts to ignore or suppress thoughts.
-The person recognizes that the obsessions are products of his or her own mind.
-There is a tendency to haggle over small details.

I know some very meticulous people, yet none of them have an obsessive-compulsive disorder. Once again, these symptoms must interfere with everyday life in order to be considered a "condition."

Everything stated above is rather, clinical. It's everything that can be seen everywhere and heard everywhere, so how does this apply to real life? The best way to relate it to real life is to tell some "real-life" stories.

First, I would like to introduce you to Stacy. Stacy's the kind of girl that everyone loves. She's the one that smiles all the time and is always so happy, outgoing, and cheerful. Stacy is that one girl that's always there to hear everyone else's problems. She's been there for every breakup, fight, depression, problem, and everything that has ever made her friends unhappy. She's the rock, the one to look up to. The truth is, behind all the smiles, happy faces, and healing words, Stacy is dying inside. She cuts herself because it's the only thing that makes her feel alive. She starves herself because she hates how she looks. She barely has a relationship with her parents, and she feels as though she's been used and abused throughout her whole life. Still, she pushes aside everything with herself when someone comes to her for help. After all, if she can't help herself, she can help others.

She's falling apart, and after years of being friends with one particular girl, she is able to open up and share the way that she truly feels, which is so far from how the world perceives her. She tells her friend Monica. This kills Monica. For years, Monica has watched Stacy be that "perfect" girl that has been there so many times when quite frankly, Monica just couldn't take it anymore. Monica must watch her hero suffer.

**What Exactly is Mental Health?**

45

But Monica has problems of her own. She is the girl that pretty much has everything. She is so talented, but humble about it all. Monica is also the rock for her friends, always being there for everyone else. But no person is perfect, and Monica, too, has her own problems. Monica has an anxiety disorder, and she lets it take over a good portion of her life. Monica also cuts herself. It's a cycle that she can never get out of, and it is destroying her. When she and Stacy talk, they realize they need to help each other, so they both give up their vices; nonetheless, they are still far from happy.

Monica wants to be there for Stacy, but it's hard, and she doesn't really know what else to do. She feels as though she can't help anymore, and she is just very worried.

Monica has another little thing that makes her, well, different. Monica has a girlfriend named Christine (talk about high school relationships being complicated). Christine's smart, pretty, and sweet, but she also suffers. She suffers from stress. The weight of the world is heavy on her shoulders, especially with school and friendships. She suffers from jealousy. She constantly worries that some friends don't really like her, and in fact, it causes her to pull away from the people around her for fear of getting hurt. She goes home and cries because she hates it, and the one person in the world she trusts with her love just can't always make it better.

Brittany is the one common friend to all of them. She listens to their problems and cares entirely too much, to the point she will worry and can not eat or sleep until she knows they are okay. Brittany suffers from an eating disorder. She knows she was never the prettiest, but she has a heart of gold. The thing is, Brittany was never overweight. She barely eats anymore, and made herself throw up a few times, and then she began to lose weight. The more she loses, the happier she feels, but it is never enough. She continues to lose weight, until it can no longer go unnoticed. Parents question if she is sick. Friends notice her frailty in hugs, yet no one approaches her. She finally goes to Stacy for help, because Stacy is the one to

Celeste Schimmenti

go to when you have a problem. Stacy stays with her night and day, and finally, Brittany is able to overcome the struggle with herself. She puts the pounds back on, but is she really happy with who she is?

Tyler is the boy that no one really likes. He has some significant friends, but other than that, he's kind of alone. No one really understands him, except one girl. She's the only one he can be himself with. Tyler wishes he had real friendships; he just never was too good at making them. Tyler's family is breaking apart, and it all can be too much to handle at times. Why won't his mother love him? One night, Tyler opened a bottle of sleeping pills and took as many as he could bear to swallow. He wished he would have died, but he did not. He isn't sure why he tried, and he regrets it now. His life is what it is, and he is who is he is; can't really change that, right?

The truth is, this isn't a story at all. These are my friends, the most important people in my life, and the stories are not just for information; they are the lives we live. These are the things we have to struggle with every day, even when no one else sees that something is wrong, and no one seems to care. When we think we are alone, we fail to recognize that others around us can relate to our feelings, often in more ways than one would hope for. We, as teenagers, will never be alone, because there are always too many people that care about us and can relate to us and share our experiences. Keeping sane is a struggle we all face, and if we face it together, there's strength in numbers.

You only get one life, and you live how you choose to. So don't get upset over the little things; don't stress over anything that's meaningless in the long-run, and never compromise your mental health for a worthless cause. Be there for the people around you because everyone needs a helping hand eventually, even if you would never expect it. Reach out, and be the strength for others who may be in a situation you were once familiar with. Keep your cool in even the toughest situations, and try your best to keep sane in your crazy fast-paced life!

**What Exactly is Mental Health?**

Celeste Schimmenti

# 6

# Astrological Sign or Life Threatening Situation?

"Something wasn't right, and from that moment on, I started to change."

*"Cancer. What is it?" you may ask. It may be an astrological sign between June twenty-first and July twenty-second, but in reality, it is a malignant growth of cells. Cancer is the cause of more than thirteen percent of all human deaths each year, affecting millions of people regardless of their age, race, religion, sex, or social status. Some cancers are inoperable; others are curable, yet hard to defeat. With the changing technology of today's modern world, new ways of curing cancer are being found. However, those who survived cancer during the twentieth century, have certain disabilities. In the following pages, you will be reading my story of a cancer survivor and my fight against the injustices due to my hearing impairment, which was brought by the heavy medication from chemotherapy.*

Many people know me as I am today, a student who excels in everything that she puts herself to, a great leader, and a wonderful, caring friend. They don't see that I am partially deaf, and if they notice that I am, they mostly assume that I was born that way. However, I wouldn't have been partially deaf if it was for this one major event in my life, where I was hospitalized for nearly a year. Behind my goal-oriented and I'll-prove-you-otherwise attitude, there is a story that I have shared with a few people in my life, which I wish to share now with all of you, even though I don't remember all of it since I was only two to three years old when it happened. It is a story that may sadden you, but to the many survivors and fighters, it may help you see that you are not alone and to never give up, no matter what the costs are. Be brave, and have faith in the future; focus on your goals, while living your life. It affects millions of people every year; however very rarely you hear of children diagnosed with a cancer. To give you a general idea of the percentage of survival for the childhood cancer I had, according to St. Jude Children's Research Hospital, in 1962, only ten percent of the children that had the cancer survived. Today, fifty-five percent survive from the same cancer.

Adrienne S. Bednarz

I had just celebrated my second birthday on September 14, as I look through the  pictures of this happy event–big balloons,  gifts, Happy Birthday banner and my cousins and friends with  smiling faces helping me to blow out candles from my birthday cake. I was adored by my parents, spoiled by my grandmother-a perfectly healthy baby. We had routines at home where my parents would leave for work everyday and my grandmother would take care of me until this one day in the middle of December. Until that day, my mother would always, trying to not wake me up, kiss the toes of my feet and in response, I would say to her, "I love you," and I would return to sleep before she would leave for work.  On that day, I got up and ran after her in the hallway asking her not to go to work. She came back home earlier, and as we were cuddling, she noticed a small bump below my left rib, under her fingers. Immediately, she called my pediatrician, but he could not comprehend what my mother was saying.  He could see me the following day, but he suggested that for her peace of mind, she should take me to the hospital.  The same night, I was taken by a friend of the family, along with Reverend Edward and my parents to the Schneider's Children Jewish Hospital in New Hyde Park, and after some tests, I was admitted.  My mother stayed with me while my father returned home.  The following morning, when my pediatrician came to the hospital, the lump had grown to the size of a grapefruit.

On Christmas Eve, the doctors confronted my parents with my diagnosis of Neuroblastoma, a cancer of the peripheral nervous tissue, with the plan to "cure" it.  The plan included six circles of gradually increased doses every 30 days of chemotherapy, two surgeries to remove the tumor and harvest bone marrow, after which came the bone marrow transplant (commonly referred to as BMT) and radiation.  I spent nine months in the hospital; in the meantime, my mother quit her job at the travel agency and stayed with me around the clock, talking to the doctors, making sure that everything was fine, and helping the nurses to look after me,

Astrological Sign or Life Threatening Situation?

while my grandmother played with me, and my father came every day after working at the Technical Career Institute and stayed late. My mother, through this entire year, helped the doctors with administering me the medication. She looked after me and made sure that I took what I needed to take at the right time. I bet some of the doctors and especially the other children might have been jealous that their mothers weren't doing the same.

Often times, she would sleep on a cot next to my bed, and let me sleep on her chest, so that I could hear the comforting beat of her heart. During these months, I only observed the change of the outside world through, the window–blooming trees with flowers in the spring turning green for the summer, before changing colors to orange, yellow and brown for the fall, and finally leaving the trees bare for the winter. It was during these nine months that I got my first color pastels and started to use a brush, with which I would paint everything in green, my favorite color. I went through chemotherapy, radiation, bone marrow transplant and surgery. My parents had to borrow money from some other friends to buy an old used van, which my mother used to drive to take me to my treatments later in the year.

Chemotherapy is the treatment of cancer with drugs that can destroy cancer cells. The drugs interfere with cell division in various possible ways. Most forms of chemotherapy target all rapidly dividing cells and are not specific for cancer cells, although some degree of specificity may come from the inability of many cancer cells to repair DNA damage, while normal cells can repair our DNA. Therefore, chemotherapy has the potential to harm healthy tissue, especially those tissues that have a high replacement rate. These cells usually replace themselves after chemotherapy. Since some drugs work better together than alone, two or more drugs are often given at the same time. During this stage, the doctors gave me the chemotherapy through a tube inserted underneath a flab of my skin in my chest. I often got sick and vomited. Because of that, I learned to associate certain smells and the way food looks to getting sick and vomiting. These taste aversions have stayed with me to this day. I often find that I will go for a food that looks good or smells good.

My treatment started out with thirty percent of chemotherapy but then increased to forty-five percent of chemotherapy. After that, I had the surgery to remove the tumor from my kidney and the bone marrow taken out. That was followed by fifty percent chemotherapy and then sixty percent. After that came the radiation and then the bone marrow put back into my lower hip.

Radiation is the use of ionizing radiation to kill cancer cells and shrink tumors. Radiation therapy can be administered externally via external beam radiotherapy or internally via brachytherapy. The effects of radiation therapy are localized and confined to the region being treated. Radiation therapy injures or destroys cells in the area being treated by damaging their genetic material, making it impossible for these cells to continue to grow and divide. Although radiation damages both cancer cells and normal cells, most normal cells can recover from the effects of radiation and function properly. The goal of radiation is to damage as many cancer cells as possible, while limiting harm to nearby healthy tissue. Therefore, it is given in many fractions, allowing healthy tissue to recover between the intervals. The radiation dose to each site depends on a number of factors, including the radiosensitivity of each cancer type and whether there are tissues and organs nearby that may be damaged by radiation. As with every other form of treatment, radiation therapy is not without its side effects. I know I had the external form of radiation, because that was the only form that existed at that time. They had to do it in order to remove the tissue during the surgery. Due to this radiation, during the surgery, they not only removed the tissue surrounding my kidney, but also my kidney as well. There was no point in keeping it, as the cancer could have spread to the kidney, or the radiation could have damaged it.

Astrological Sign or Life Threatening Situation?

I also had a bone marrow transplant, which is taking either a donor's bone marrow, or your own bone marrow, before chemotherapy starts, and freezing it. After you are done with the treatment, they insert the bone marrow back. It usually takes a week before the white blood cell and the platelet counts are back up. Do you know that the white blood cells, the foundation of your immune system, are the first to come up, and they double everyday? Do you know that in many cases, the doctors like to give the bone marrow of the opposite gender to the patient, because it is a faster indicator of whether the bone marrow was accepted or not? The doctors in the BMT wing of Schneider's Children's Hospital took my own bone marrow from my back, in the area near the tailbone. They froze that bone marrow, and for some amount of time, kept it. Once I was through a major part of my treatment, they returned the bone marrow to me. The reason that they did that was because chemotherapy destroys cells, and therefore lowered my immune system. If they had not taken out my healthy bone marrow, I would have lost my immune system after chemotherapy.

I finally got my 100 percent chemotherapy dose, which wiped my immune system completely. Due to the low immune system, I had to stay in the bubble room. The only thing I recall from that place was that it was a bare room, with a plastic curtain on the right side of my bed. The curtain had a hole, through which visitors could talk to me without actually hurting me. During this time, my visitors were only close family, and Roni, who would come and play with me as she did before I went to the bubble room. The only difference was that she could only bring her sterilized games. These visitors had to go through the sterilizing room, and go through the same procedures that the surgeon goes before surgery. They could stay with me only two hours, before they left and scrubbed themselves again. Back then, my visitors had to wear a yellow cap, gown and slippers when they stood behind the curtains. However, if they wished to pass the curtains, they had to change into the blue caps, gowns and slippers that the hospital

Adrienne S. Bednarz

supplied them. The room was sterilized four times a day, so that the bacteria would not attack my low immune system and get me sick. It could be fatal if I got sick with such a low immune system. But I ended up getting sick anyway, because I received red rashes, and no one could figure out why I was sick. Then there was a young doctor who checked me and said that I had chicken pox. So the entire hospital went into an uproar, and sterilized all of the rooms, hallways, and bathrooms, because of me. Therefore, in a strange way, I became a mini-celebrity inside the hospital.

Around Christmas time, the US Air company sponsored a trip to the North Pole for cancer children. So my mother, father and grandmother went on the "trip." I remember, as my mother and I boarded the plane for a few hours, while my father and my grandmother stayed at the airport. While the plane drove around John F. Kennedy Airport, it started to snow outside, and I really thought that we had landed at the North Pole. I was very excited to see Santa Claus and ask him for some gifts. As we came off the plane and entered through the gate, elves met us in their green garments, candy cane socks, and jingling hats and shoes. They were very kind and quite huggable; I wanted to take one home with me. The entire gate was transformed into Santa's place—it was barely recognizable as the airport—and so I thought we landed right at Santa's doorstep. I remember that I ended up getting a stuffed white cat (which was longer than me at the time), and a green unicorn which allowed me to braid its hair and tail. Throughout this entire trip, "Good Morning America" was taping us, and I ended up on TV (without realizing it).

At the time of my illness, no one was thinking about the side effects of chemotherapy. The most important thing was to bring me to remission. When you think about the side effects, you usually think about the weight loss due to loss of appetite, or the loss of hair. But these are just the immediate effects of chemotherapy. I have seen chemotherapy affect kids so that they lost their mobility, and had to learn to walk again. I have seen kids who have lost their memories to the extent that they could not even remember their names due to the chemotherapy.  Those are some reversible long term effects of chemotherapy.  I considered myself a lucky one –I had done well through the treatment, but the effects of the chemotherapy let themselves be known later in my life.  I had lost my high frequency hearing, so that I cannot hear the birds singing, but I will hear a phone on vibrate ringing across the room.  People sometimes assume that I am ignoring them when they are talking to me.  The trick is that sometimes I do not hear what they are saying, because I'm too focused on something that I am doing.  They have to get my full attention so that I can focus on them, and face me, so that I could lip read what they are saying along with my hearing aids to interact with this world.  I can not simply split my attention, like some, to listen to someone talking, while doing something on the computer.  The loss of hearing as a long term effect is minor compared to a life lost due to cancer.  As much attention as I got from the staff in my time at the hospital, the return to the real world had been tough.  The truth of the matter, as I narrated in the passages above, is that people can not cope with illness.  They either turn away their heads because they are scared or they are mean; however, I never was contagious.

When I entered kindergarten, I didn't know how to speak English. That was my major challenge during my elementary years; however, on top of that, in third grade, I got my first hearing aids.  I was bewildered when my mother took me for hearing testing, only to find that it wasn't like it should be.  But I was even more upset when I got those metal "things" on my ears because I didn't understand what was going on around me.  The one thing that I realized was that I was going to be a lot different then everyone else, and that it would give them more reason to pick on me.  At the Overlook Hospital, I remember hiding behind my mother and crying as we entered the waiting room to get my grandmother, who was waiting for us.  At that time, my grandmother was my only source of comfort, as she patted my head, and said, "It is going to be all

Adrienne S. Bednarz

56

right," in Polish. After that, my teachers at school were so happy that I got hearing aids saying, "Oh, now she is going to be able to perform better," especially when I got the microphone, that allowed me to channel the teacher's voice alone. However, the microphone got very annoying, because throughout the years, my teachers kept forgetting that they had it on, and would often leave the classroom to talk with other teachers or students in the hallways. So guess what?....I ended up hearing *every single word* of those "private" conversations.

Other students used to jeer at me; often times I heard, "Oh, look there's the deaf girl," and "She's stupid." Therefore, I made very few friends during my elementary years, and I became introverted—silent as a mouse. I detested speaking in front of classes, and barely spoke to anyone unless they asked me a question. I was constantly sad and depressed during those years because I wanted to be liked by everyone. It put a lot of stress on me, which I channeled into homework. By the time I reached Kawameeh Middle School, things didn't click anymore. It didn't make sense that those students who called ME stupid didn't get on the Honors Roll in Central Five. If I was the "stupid" one, then why was I on the first honor roll all the time in Central Five; and why did *I* receive the Presidential Award that year? Something wasn't right, and from that moment on, I started to change. I had gotten out of the Resource Center by the time I was in sixth grade and entered classes with in-class support. It was soon clear that I didn't need it because I was very independent and focused in my studies. I was also happy with getting out of the Resource Center, simply because I detested that place. I didn't think I learned much from it, and on top of that, the teachers were a bit rude. My confidence mounted as I entered seventh grade, because that was the year that I had all regular classes, *and* I got rid of the microphone because I wasn't using it anymore. I had stopped bothering to even go to the nurse to pick it up; it had gotten too frustrating to deal with. I was still overly self-conscious, and my carrying a small green Easter basket, which

Astrological Sign or Life Threatening Situation?

held my microphone, did not boost my confidence at all. Often times, I left it in my locker, or if I had it with me, it stayed on the floor with my books; from time to time, I gave it to my teachers.

By the time I graduated middle school, I was already starting to not care about what people said. "Let them say what they wish about me. I love myself for who I am, and who I've been; they don't matter." I thought to myself. Some day I was sure that I was going to have friends that mattered, but at that point in time, I needed to focus on my school work so that I could get ahead. Throughout my eighth grade, one of my teacher's sons had cancer, and I ended up telling her my story, as well as supporting them. I don't know how much I helped, but showing support to someone who is going through hard times is very important. It shows people that you care, and that there are others in the world like them—suffering through the same thing they are.

I entered Union High School with two honors classes—history and science—which was a drastic change in such a short time. But I managed to succeed in both classes. And it wasn't long before I found my new best friend—someone who cared about me, and mattered to me, just like I cared about her and mattered to her. I met Alysse Selby on the first day of high school on the school bus. I remember that she had a big pink backpack that looked heavy, and her hair was in two pigtails. I asked her if I could sit down, seeing as there were no other seats, and she agreed. Soon enough, we were talking, and we learned each other's histories.

People prefer to affiliate themselves with achievers, not losers. I was like every other kid in my age group–wanting to play with my classmates, to have friends, be likable; instead, I was pushed away because I was different. Why? Imagine this scene: You are on the playground, and you want to play with the kids, but you hear a child say to another, "Don't play with her because she is deaf," and pulling the other child away by the hand. How would you feel? These kind of things hurt a lot, especially when you are a child. After all, a child is so young,

Adrienne S. Bednarz

and they do not have a shield made out of metal. No one ever does, but a child's shield is thinner and weaker than a sheet of paper. These types of events leave scars that go more than just skin deep; they leave scars in you heart, scars that never heal. In turn, these scars are permanent reminders of the pain these people caused, and pain sometimes makes you aggressive. Now you know why many handicapped people are mean. They tend to push people away, because that is the only self defense mechanism that they ever know, so that they would not get hurt.

From Resource Center, extra help teachers and speech classes in sixth grade, to graduating high school with Advanced Placement classes, I came a long way, working hard. I am confident, and I am proud of who I am. Even though, I am still registered with the state as a disabled person, I am not qualified for any public assistance because of the performance in my classes–honors and Advanced Placement. I am taking the same workload and the same tests like a lot of the students, but I have to work twice as hard as the others. I know that I am different, but it does not hold me back from what I am doing, and what I want to do. I have learned a lot from these years. Don't be afraid to stand out in a crowd; just because you're different in some way, you shouldn't be accepted. You're never alone, no matter what happens to you. There have been many who went through something like this and many more may be going through it right now. If you know something about what that person is going through— reach out to them. Being sad and sorry for oneself doesn't help teenagers or adults—it may lead to suicide. Being mentally healthy, makes you physically healthy, and leads to a long life of happiness. Live for the future, and laugh a lot; let go of the past, and let those scars heal. They eventually will.

Astrological Sign or Life Threatening Situation?

**Adrienne S. Bednarz**

# 7

# What Should I Eat?

Teenagers today have a great deal on their minds. They must answer important questions about what colleges they will attend, what occupations they are most suited for, and whether their shoes match their outfits. Such key issues are often teenagers' top priorities. The subject of nutrition is frequently overlooked or outright ignored. As a result, many teenagers eat very poorly. Often, they choose satisfying taste over nutritional value. A contributing factor to this common mistake is a lack of foresight on the part of the teenager. One can easily forget at such a young age that one's body must last the entirety of his or her life. This forgetfulness causes many teenagers to eat unhealthy foods that will lead to obesity and diseases- such as diabetes- later in life. However, there is another reason for some teenagers' bad eating habits. Teens just do not know what they should be eating. Fortunately, the Food and Drug Administration has arrived to save the day. Actually, the FDA has saved many lives through extensive research and stringent regulations on the products available to consumers. However, one does not need to know all of the FDA's responsibilities. One must only know the FDA's guidelines for a healthy diet.

Some aspects of healthy living are common knowledge. For example, eating chocolate cake for every meal is not good for one's health. Also, some exercise is better than no exercise, and a lot of exercise is probably best. However, there are many important aspects of a good diet of which many people are unaware. As a result, the FDA created what are known as Recommended Dietary Allowances. The Recommended Dietary Allowances (RDA) are basically ideal amounts of the different food groups that a person should include in his or her diet. There are five food groups. The three best groups are the grain, vegetable, and fruit groups. The FDA recommends that a person eat six to eleven servings of grain products, three to five servings of vegetables, and two to four servings of fruit each day. A person should also consume two to three servings of the dairy group and two to three servings of the meat and bean group each day. The FDA also

Vincent Michael Imbornone

recommends avoiding foods high in fat and sugar content that provide little to no nutrients. As the author can attest, avoiding such foods is no small feat.

Knowing the number of servings of each group is a good start to a healthy lifestyle; however, this information does not mean much if a person does not know what is considered one serving. One slice of bread or an ounce of cereal is considered one serving of grain. Also, half of a cup of pasta or rice is a serving of grain. One serving of vegetables is equal to a cup of raw, leafy vegetables. Half a cup of cooked or chopped vegetables or three-fourths of a cup of vegetable juice is a serving of vegetables. One piece of fruit- such as an apple- is a serving. Half a cup of chopped, cooked, or canned fruit is also a serving, as is three-fourths of a cup of fruit juice. One serving of the milk group can be attained in the form of a cup of milk or yogurt, an ounce and a half of natural cheese, or two ounces of processed cheese. The final food group is the meat and beans group. One serving can be attained in a large variety of ways. Two to three ounces of lean meat, poultry, or fish is a serving. An egg, half of a cup of cooked beans, or a third of a cup of nuts are equivalent to an ounce of meat. Eating all of the recommended foods in the right proportions ensures that a person is consuming a healthy amount of nutrients. However, the best way to get all of the necessary nutrients out of one's diet is by varying the foods a person eats from each food group.

Often people rely on supplements to provide the nutrients necessary for a healthy diet. However, if a person eats the recommended foods in the proper quantities, nutritional supplements are not necessary. Actually, taking the supplement may cause a person to attain too much of a particular nutrient, thus making that supplement detrimental to one's health. Also, a supplement cannot replace a proper diet. The only way to meet one's nutritional needs is by eating healthy foods in the amounts specified by the FDA.

There are certain minerals and nutrients that are very important to a person's diet. One important necessity of a good diet is calcium. Calcium is necessary for strong bones. It is especially important to adolescents, whose bones are growing and developing. There are many possible sources of calcium. Milk group foods are very good sources of calcium. Dark-green, leafy vegetables, tofu, tortillas, sardines, anchovies, and salmon are also good sources of calcium. However, some have high fat content, which should be avoided.

Iron is an important part of a person's diet. Iron can be found in foods from the meat group. However, one must be careful to avoid the high levels of fat that these foods contain. Leafy greens, legumes, and whole wheat breads are also good sources of iron.

Eating the proper foods is an important component of good health; however, the FDA also recommends that a person get regular physical exercise. A person should get at least thirty minutes of physical activity per day. One should exercise every day of the week if possible. There are a number of different activities that will suffice. For example, a person can jog, walk, dance, or play a sport. Activities, such as mowing the lawn, gardening, or cleaning the house can also serve as physical activity. Physical activity is important to one's health, but it is also a good way to maintain one's weight. Being overweight can create a number of health problems that will follow a teen for the rest of his or her life. It is best to practice healthy eating habits and get the proper amount of exercise early in one's life. As a person gets older, he or she becomes more set in his or her ways. Change becomes difficult as a result. It is especially difficult to begin exercising later in life. As a person becomes older, one generally has less energy and is less capable of physical activity. If a person gets into ideal shape as a teenager, strenuous exercise will be easier later in life, assuming that teenager continues to maintain his or her good habits.

In addition to avoiding excess weight, a person should pay close attention to where excess weight is located. Excess weight in the abdomen is the most adverse to one's health. If

Vincent Michael Imbornone

a person has too much weight there, he or she should exercise more to reduce it. Excess weight in places such as the hips and thighs is not as bad for one's health. A good way to avoid abdominal fat is by frequently measuring one's waist. If it is out of proportion to the rest of one's body, then there is clearly a problem.

Unfortunately, some people regulate their body weights to such an extreme extent that they develop eating disorders. One should decide what his or her ideal weight is solely by looking at one's appearance. A person should base one's weight on the normal range as recommended by the Food and Drug Administration. However, the best way to ensure that one is the proper weight is to eat the proper foods and get thirty minutes of exercise per day. This is much more effective than trying to limit the amount of food one eats to unhealthily low amounts or going on unusual diets that eliminate one of the important food groups.

An influential factor affecting body weight and health is calorie intake. A diet light in calories but low in vitamins and essential nutrients is likely to result in obesity and other illnesses. Avoid calories by eating food with little fat or sugar. A diet with few calories would emphasize grains, fruits, and vegetables. Meat and poultry, which have a large amount of fat, should be eaten much more sparingly. To fully understand the value of eating less fat, one must learn the impact that consuming fat has o one's calorie intake. For example, based on a 2,000-calorie diet, a person should get 600 calories from fat at the most. 600 calories would be produced by eating 65 grams of fat. If one knows how many grams of fat are in his or her food, that person can estimate the calories of the fat by multiplying by nine.

Although people should avoid fatty foods in general, it is particularly important that people avoid saturated fats. Understanding the dangers of saturated fats is most easily accomplished once one understands saturated fat molecules. The term "saturated" in the phrase "saturated fats" refers to the hydrogen in the tails of fat molecules. A fatty acid tail in a fat molecule is saturated if all of the carbon atoms form single bonds with neighboring carbon atoms. The carbon atoms can only from single bonds due to the presence of hydrogen, which binds to all of the carbon atoms. Because the maximum number of hydrogen atoms is bonded to the chain of carbon atoms, the fatty acid tail is saturated with hydrogen, hence the name. It is not the hydrogen atoms themselves that are bad for one's health. The shape of the fatty acid, which is a result of the hydrogen atoms, makes saturated fats bad for a person's health. Saturation causes the tails of fat molecules to be perfectly straight. As a result, the fat molecules can align and from a solid very easily at a high temperature. The erratic shape of unsaturated fats prevents them from fitting together well at high temperatures. That particular characteristic of saturated fats causes them to solidify in one's blood vessels. This can have a number of dangerous consequences, including heart attack or stroke.

A food, such as butter, contains saturated fats, which is why butter is solid at room temperature. Olive oil and other vegetable oils generally contain unsaturated fats. As a result, they are liquid at room temperature. Fats from meat and milk are saturated. The Food and Drug Administration recommends that a person limit his or her saturated fats to only ten percent of the total calories in his or her diet. Unsaturated fats in vegetable oils, nuts, and fish are much better for one's health. These fats are able to reduce one's cholesterol level, rather than increase it. Trans fats, although better than saturated fats, should be replaced with unsaturated fats if possible.

Cholesterol is another dangerous substance that people should avoid. Excessive amounts of cholesterol are very bad for one's health. Because the human body produces its own cholesterol, any cholesterol consumed results in excess cholesterol in the blood stream. The FDA recommends that a person consume 300 milligrams of cholesterol or less each day. Cholesterol is found mostly in meat, milk, fish, and egg

Vincent Michael Imbornone

yolks. Avoiding these foods is a good way to reduce one's intake of cholesterol.

Sugars are other substances that should be consumed in moderation. Sugars exist in a variety of forms. There are simple sugars known as monosaccharides. There are also complex sugars, known as polysaccharides, which are composed of multiple monosaccharides that are bonded together. After digestion, all sugars are broken down into monosaccharides, which are then broken down to an even greater extent if necessary. Cellulose, a polysaccharide known at fiber, is not digested. Sugars have been linked to diabetes and hyperactivity. However, research shows that consumption of large amounts of sugar does not contribute to those problems. Diabetes is usually the result of being overweight. Sugars can be found in fruits, vegetables, milk, and breads. If a person's diet contains large amounts of sugar, he or she should pay particular attention to dental hygiene. Sugars can stick to teeth and promote tooth decay.

People should consume sodium in moderation. Sodium and sodium chloride, known as salt, are commonly used to process food or add flavor. Consuming too much sodium can result in high blood pressure. To reduce the likelihood of having high blood pressure, one should consume salt and sodium sparingly.

Another dietary concern that affects teenagers is alcohol consumption. If the law has not convinced a teenager not to drink, it is not likely that the FDA will fare much better. In addition to the law prohibiting alcohol consumption by people under the age of twenty-one, the Food and Drug Administration advises that adolescents should not drink. However, adolescents do drink. Why shouldn't adolescents be included in all of the excitement of drinking? What could possibly be more fun than dizziness, headaches, vomiting, and memory loss? To put it simply, many teenagers do not take that advice. If they don't, they should limit their alcohol consumption to one drink per day. A drink can be twelve ounces of beer, five ounces of wine, or one and half ounces of eighty-proof whiskey. Also, alcohol should always be consumed with food.

The Food and Drug Administration's recommendations can be summarized in a few key ideas. First, people of all ages should get regular exercise. Second, people should eat foods rich in vitamins and minerals while avoiding foods with large amounts of fat. It is most important that a person avoid saturated fats and trans fats because of their tendencies to accumulate in blood vessels, which restricts blood flow. The easiest way to consume a healthy amount of nutrients and fats would be by eating mostly grains, fruits, and vegetables. Meat, fish, and poultry are often good sources of protein and should be consumed in moderation. Third, people should avoid sodium, sugar, and other foods with no nutritional benefits. Finally, the best way to maintain one's weight and keep it within a healthy range is by eating properly, exercising, and following the Food and Drug Administration's recommendations. A person can easily monitor his or her intake of fat or calories due to the labels placed on food as a result of the Food and Drug Administration. Generally, a 2,000-calorie diet is best. However, people with greater energy needs can consume more calories. Those calories should not be attained through fat but by sugars, which are also known as carbohydrates. Eating healthy foods and getting exercise are not activities reserved for older people. It is important that people begin these activities at a young age so they will be able to continue them for the remainders of their lives. In addition, when determining the contents of one's diet, one should always keep in mind the importance of moderation.

Vincent Michael Imbornone

# 8

# I Don't Get Enough Sleep... So What?

"Sleep is food for your brain! And like food, sleep is not an option; it is a necessity for survival and development."

Did you know...?

-If it takes you less than five minutes to fall asleep at night, this means you're sleep deprived.
-After five nights of only four hours of sleep, three drinks will have the same effect on your body as six would when you've slept adequately.
-Teenagers need as much sleep as small children (about ten hours)
-The extra-hour of sleep received when clocks are put back at the start of daylight in Canada has been found to coincide with a fall in the number of road accidents.
-Sleep deprivation causes acne.
-Sleep debt can contribute to obesity

## The Big Picture

It is without a doubt that teenagers are notorious for keeping late nights. But to you it is justifiable, right? You're busy with school, sports, extra-curricular activities, homework, job, and many more. Definitely, a good night's sleep is not your utmost priority. Perhaps you don't think you need much sleep; "I can manage with five hours of sleep!" (Borkowski and Dowshen). or maybe you reason you can make it all up in the weekend. "Besides, I always sleep until noon on Saturday!" (Borkowski and Dowshen).

The average teen requires at least nine hours of sleep every night. Researchers also revealed that the average teen only gets 7.3 hours of sleep per night, and a staggering 26% of the teens studied received 6.5 hours or less! Many teenagers do not realize the value and significance of sleep. Sleep is extremely important. From your health, to your personality and to your academic performance, sleep highlights and affects your teenager years, and this becomes a vicious cycle for the rest of your life.

Why do we need to sleep anyway?

Although I am a very active person who enjoys performing many activities, the one activity and pleasure I

Oluwatosin Oluyadi

70

enjoy most is sleeping. Words cannot describe how I just love to rest my head and drift into la-la land. No matter how much work I have to do, I still make sure I get at least eight hours of sleep every night. When I tell my friends I go to bed at ten o'clock, they look at me like I am speaking a Martian language. They often ask how I get so much sleep when there are so many assignments to be completed. But the question I should really ask them is; "Why is it strange to go to bed at this time?" Why is doing assignments any more important than your health? After all, how would you do your daily assignment if you did not have your health?

<u>The Inside Story</u>

Some the reasons teenagers keep late nights is they really do not understand the pure significance of sleep. Sleep is not simply the opposite of being awake. It is surprising the large amounts of brain activity that occurs while you are in sweet slumber. As you sleep, your brain travels through important stages. Sleep is food for your brain! And like food, sleep is not an option; it is a necessity for survival and development.

Many teenagers believe that if they don't get enough sleep during the week, they can catch up on their sleep during the short weekend, and their sleeping cycle will be back to normal. But it is not that easy! Trying to pay back your sleep "debt" on weekends doesn't always work.

As a senior in high school, I have a lot on my plate this year (college applications, Advance Placement Classes, and Scholarships; just to name a few!). I find myself sleeping a little later than I am used to doing. But then I reassure myself with the thought, "I'll make up for my sleep on the weekend." This is one of the worst things I could do to myself. I began to feel unusually exhausted during the weekdays, and I find myself wanting to go to bed at eight o'clock. That was when I knew I needed to get hold of my sleep pattern before it becomes a vicious cycle.

I Don't Get Enough Sleep...So What?

One of the most important stages of sleep is REM (Rapid Eye Movement) sleep, or more simply, the dream stage. This is when your mind processes your learning and experiences and helps you adjust to the world around you. REM sleep usually happens after you've already been asleep for about four hours. If you only sleep for a measly six hours every night, and you use naps or weekends to make it up, you are not receiving the same quality of sleep that you would have if you had that valuable extra two hours

The human body is a strong element, but it is also very delicate. There is a time for work, and there is a time for rest. It is not a machine that can function continuously. When you begin to deprive your body from adequate sleep, you will eventually pay. The human body is a selfish being. It thrives on good health and care. If the body does not get what it deserves, rather than your continuing to self-destruct, the body shuts itself down in defense.

Sleep serves not only a restorative function for developing bodies and brains, but it is also an important time when you process and contemplate on what you learned throughout the day. There is a strong correlation between the amount of sleep you get and your academic performance. I never understand why my friends will stay up all night studying for a test. They will come to school with bloodshot eyes, tired and anxious. They go through this torture in order to achieve a good test grade. But what they do not understand is there is an optimal capacity at which your brain can study and assimilate information. After this level is attained, no amount of hours staring at a textbook will get you a higher grade. It is like pouring water into a bucket with a hole at the bottom. It gets you nowhere! In fact, it does you more harm than good. The irony of the whole situation is I get the same result (even better at times) than these people that spend all night studying.

Oluwatosin Oluyadi

If you do not put your health as a primary priority, it is inevitable that they will suffer the repercussions. In the same manner that you make sure you getting enough food in your stomach, good sleep habits are an essential part of staying healthy and more importantly, being happy. I know you are probably used to the nagging voices of parents and teachers telling you to get some sleep, but they are right. If you want to perform well on tests, play sports without falling flat on your face, and hang out with your friends without turning into a zombie or getting tweaked at everything they say, you will need to develop a sleep routine.

But I am a teenager, I don't fall asleep as well as I used to...

This is understandable. When children reach adolescence, their circadian rhythms ( which are biological internal clocks that regulate sleep patterns) tend to deviate, causing teenagers to naturally feel more conscious and alert later at night and wake up later in the morning. This nature, "phase delay"(Carpenter) can make it difficult for them to fall asleep before eleven at night. "In the competition between the natural tendency to stay up late and early school start times, a teen's sleep is what loses out." ("Teens Not Getting").

Just because your body naturally keeps you up later than usual does not mean you have add to it. You can help yourself and make sure you are ready for bed at the appropriate times. You could start with eliminating the late cell-phone call (you can definitely do without them). Try to peel yourself away from the television in the hour you are preparing for bed. You are just bombarding your sensitive eyes with the unnecessary light, making it more difficult to fall asleep. Trust me, if your day is as eventful as mine, you will be out like a candle before you know it.

Sleeping disorder...Are you a victim?

I Don't Get Enough Sleep...So What?

Some teenagers may not realize it but they could be suffering from chronic sleeping disorders, especially when you are constantly becoming tired and, emotionally unstable at awkward times of the day.  If you experience any of the following symptoms do not hesitate to consult you doctor. You've got to nip the problem in the bud!

Sleepwalking is when you walk or move around during sleep. Most sleepwalkers don't sleepwalk very often.  As a result, it usually doesn't become a serious problem. But some sleepwalkers move around almost every night, and they are at risk of getting hurt if they go into the kitchen where there are sharp items, or even worse, if they venture outside.

Sleep apnea is a disorder that causes a person to stop breathing temporarily during sleep. Causes of apnea include enlarged adenoids (tissues located in the passage that connects the nose and throat) and tonsils and obesity. A person with sleep apnea may experience snoring, difficulty breathing, choking, and heavy sweating during sleep. Other symptoms include feeling extremely sleepy or irritable during the day.

Insomnia occurs when you have a lot of trouble falling asleep, especially when it happens frequently. The most common cause for insomnia is stress caused by a big change in habitual activities, such as starting at a new school or moving houses. Chronic insomnia lasts more than a month and may be caused by problems such as depression.

Narcolepsy is a sleep disorder in which the person has sleep "attacks" during the day during which she can't stay awake no matter how much sleep she has gotten the night before. Narcolepsy can be dangerous because people with it can fall asleep in dangerous situations, such as while driving a car.

Helpful Tips in achieving good sleep routines

It is high-time you take control of your life, and this means taking control of your health.  If you are not healthy, you will soon realize that life will just pass you by, and there is nothing you can do about it. However, like any bad habits in life, it is never too late to turn over a new leaf and establish good sleeping patterns. Although this will prove to be extremely difficult at first, it is certainly not impossible. Your parents will also be of great significance during this period of readjustment. Let them help you! Make them a part of your sleeping routines.

Although these precautions listed below may seem rather simple and may prove to be ineffective at first, it is disciplining yourself to stick to this routine that truly is the difficult task.

Make sleeping your #1 priority. Get into the right set of mind that sleep is the most important thing in your day. Once you have fully established and honestly committed to this thought, you would soon see that everything would begin to smoothen out.

Set a reasonable bed time, and stick to it! Although this may be easy to plan out, it is the hardest to follow. Many teenagers make good plans for themselves, but a number of them do not actually follow these plans. Regulating your sleeping pattern is very important. You would even be surprised at how much work and personal activities you could still achieve and still get a good night sleep. Because you are putting pressure on yourself, you are forced to do your work at the right time, leaving no room for procrastination. Also, try to stay on schedule, even if it's a weekend. Don't go to sleep more than an hour later or wake up more than two to three hours later than usual.

Avoid long naps. If you are drowsy during the day, a 30-minute nap after school may be revitalizing. But too long a nap (which really is not nap anymore) further distorts your sleeping cycles.

Detoxify all caffeine contents in your body. A shot of caffeine may help you stay awake during class, but the effects are fleeting. Why put yourself through torture by giving your body rapid burst of energy only for it to dwindle even lower few hours later? It would be more reasonable if you have constant levels of energy throughout the day.

Go with the flow. If you are feeling like time is not on your side, do not stress out and panic. That is the worst thing you can do. Just go with the flow! Whatever you can achieve is your limit and capacity. Tomorrow is another day. Would you not rather face it with a clear head?

Maybe after this long discussion, you will be more obliged to treat your body to a well-deserved sleep. Sleep doesn't just revitalize you physically, but it also revives you mentally. It keeps you emotionally stable. You are fully armed and ready to take on life by its horns! Why shouldn't we all want this feeling? Sleep should be your reward for an exhausting day. There should be no debate in your mind as to whether you should get some sleep or not. Just sleep. You deserve it!

# 9

# Exercise: What's the Point?

"I hurt in places I didn't even know existed...it changed my life"

Exercise, by definition, is to engage in physical activity to sustain or improve physical fitness. By definition, exercise can surely sound boring. From an early age, teachers, parents, coaches, and doctors talk about how important it is to stay fit and exercise regularly. To make sure this need for physical fitness is met, many children are enrolled in a gym class, or signed up to play a sport. To me, this sounds more like a punishment than a method for improving your lifestyle.

I have always tried to be athletic. When I was younger, my parents signed me up for gymnastics classes and soccer teams to keep me active and involved. Unfortunately for all of us, I was not the most coordinated gymnast or the most talented soccer player on the team; once I yelled from the field for my mother to buy me a snack from the ice cream truck. These two were not for me. At that point in my young life, attending practices, competitions, and games were not enjoyable; maintaining an exercise routine was like torture.

After my first few attempts at sports failed, to keep me exercised and healthy I tried cheerleading, figure skating, field hockey, and softball, each only lasting me a few seasons; I just could not find something I truly enjoyed. I found that if I was not enjoying my exercise, I was not really benefiting from it. Sure, physically I was fit, but mentally I was becoming stressed and unfulfilled. I realized that the exercise I was getting meant nothing if I dragged myself to practice, complained afterwards, and dreaded going to games on the weekends.

With this new notion in my head, I finished my last season of field hockey and tried something new; horseback riding. As a young girl I always loved horses, and I was very interested in taking riding lessons. Nothing ever came out of my interest in equines except a few pony rides here and there, or a trip to the local stables to watch the riders and their trusty steeds. After years of failed attempts at finding an enjoyable form of exercise, I decided I would give it one last try; I told my parents I wanted to take horseback riding lessons.

Looking at my track record...I was probably going to love everything about riding from the beginning, get into the

Kristen Murdoch

sport for a few months, and give up again. Fortunately, this time it was different. When I was thirteen years old, I sat on my first horse, an old grey gelding named Class Act. Honestly, I did not enjoy myself very much. I saw the other girls in the ring trotting, cantering, and jumping around and was jealous I could barely get old Classy to walk where I wanted him to. By the end of my first ride, I was discouraged; horseback riding was certainly not as easy as I thought it would be. This huge, two thousand pound animal was not going to just do what I wanted it do. That night I complained that my seat bones hurt from the saddle, my spirits were slightly crushed, and I had muscle aches in muscles I did not even know existed. Imagine my parents' surprise when I said I wanted to go back the next week!

Something about horseback riding sucked me in that day Classy and I ambled around the riding ring. Something in the back of my mind told me to keep going, and guess what? I did. I have been riding and competing in the world of equestrian sports for five years now, and I love everything about it. My seat bones have now grown accustomed to the feel of a saddle beneath me, and the pain from my first ride is nonexistent. Even when things go wrong, I know I can improve, and those muscles I did not know existed? They are now some of the most developed muscles in my body. Horseback riding was, and is, the exercise of my dreams.

With horseback riding, it did not matter if I could score a goal, run backwards down a field to chase a ball, or flip over backwards. The only thing that mattered was my own personal achievement and position while riding each lesson. Heels down; shoulders back; chest open; eyes up/ seat in the saddle. Finally! Something I could do by myself. My happiness, after realizing this, accounted for my enthusiasm and willingness to progress right off the bat with this sport. Riding did not come to me in a week, but I knew that with practice, training, and dedication, one day it would.

My dream exercise has also leant its benefits to two other sports that have become important in my life; cross country and track. Because of the way I fell in love with horseback riding, in the off-season I wanted to find ways to keep up with my exercise regimen and stay on top of my game and my progress. Riding really built up my leg muscles, and someone I ride with suggested I give the cross country team a try. If nothing else, it would build my muscle endurance, and if I really didn't like it, the season only lasts from September to November. Towards the end of my sophomore year in high school, I signed up for the team.

Much to my surprise, I got a call in July from my captain asking when I could start practice. Practice? During my summer vacation? Surely this girl was kidding! Oh no...no she was not. At my first day of practice, I showed up with my bright white new running shoes; every veteran runner on the team knew I was new to this. As we set off to run our first mile (FIRST mile?!), I could see the girls breaking off in to groups.

"You new girls can stick in the back and just follow us," one girl said, looking back. "If you can't make it, just turn around and wait for us to finish around here."

That was it. I was not about to let myself be categorized as a newbie who couldn't keep up! My stubbornness took over, and luckily, my riding built up the muscles I needed to run, because I took off and caught up with the middle pack of girls; some were seniors that had been running since middle school! We completed not just one, but two miles that day. Like last time, I came home sore, tired, and ready to go back for more. By the end of my first cross country season, I was running third on my team and scoring points at the big races.

Running proved to be another excellent form of exercise that I actually enjoyed taking part in. Cross country season turned into winter track season, and winter track into spring. I still kept up with my riding, and between the two sports, I was in the best shape, mentally and physically, of my life thus-far. As I became more involved with both running and horseback riding, my overall level of satisfaction with myself increased. My muscles were toned, my lungs were healthy, I had more leg muscle than I knew what to do with, and both sports provided

Kristen Murdoch

me with a core group of friends I knew I could count on, even when we were not riding or running. Becoming involved with horseback riding and running brought me together with a group of my peers I would not have known otherwise. We all share a passion for the same sport, yet we have our own unique qualities. When we all come together we are certainly a motley crew, but it works for us.

The friends I have met through pursuing different types of exercise have become some of the most trustworthy, reliable, and all around greatest people I have ever met. Our shared passion for a single thing brings us close as a group, and individual interests besides them allow us to form intimate friendships. Because of the way I felt about myself when exercising, and the amazing group of people I was surrounded with, I never wanted practice sessions or competitions to end.

Unfortunately, during what would become my last season of track, I started to get terrible knee pains, the result of a bad fall off of a horse over a jump the previous winter. After tests and x-rays, my orthopedist found that I had shattered a layer of cartilage in my left knee, and it was unable to repair properly because of overuse. I was able to finish out the season, but my doctor recommended I stop the heavy competition and fast paced miles I had grown to love. I was crushed that I could no longer run with my team.

Luckily, I was able to keep up with my riding, despite being sidelined on the track. Almost immediately after I stopped running, though, I could feel myself losing my fitness. Even though I was riding every day, and exercising those muscles, the ones that I had developed from only running were beginning to go away. The 5:55 miles I used to pride myself on being able to complete seemed like I would never get there again.

After developing an incredibly vigorous stretching and warm up routine, I was able to run again without much pain. I won't be returning to the relay team any time soon, but I can run my own distances comfortably. I took exercising for

Exercise: What's the Point?

granted a lot in my life. I realized that in order to maintain a safe routine, I needed to exercise before exercising.

Since I was always shuffling from one sport to another, I figured there would always be something I was able to do, and that I would find a lot I could stick with and enjoy in many ways. Although there are many things, now, that I enjoy doing, I found my true favorite forms of exercise, and when I cannot do them, I am crushed. There is nothing I look forward to more each day than the end of my last class, so I can go to the barn, saddle up my horse, and ride until we are both tired.

Finding the kind of exercise that suits you is the key factor in becoming active, and reaping all of the benefits of exercise. Once I was able to find an activity that I loved to do, it acted as a gateway to more activities, and more ways to better myself. Sticking to my exercise "programs" has taught me about prioritizing, hard work, dedication, competition, self-fulfillment, and most of all, believing in myself.

If I did not believe that I could one day ride as well as the other girls in the ring that day with Class Act, I would never have come back for more. That old stubborn grey horse taught me more than any teacher in a classroom ever has and probably ever will. Sitting on his flea-bitten colored back, I discovered a form of exercise that would become a passion that would eventually consume most of my life. Without believing that I could ride that silly old horse, I would have never seen the need to take up running either.

When you exercise you are free to set your own goals, whether you are in a competition environment or doing sit-ups on your bedroom floor. Each time you reach one of those goals, an indescribable feeling comes over you. You know you have succeeded, you know you have won, you know you can do it again, and you know next time you will work even harder to do it better than before.

Not only will you feel good from exercising, but you will look just as good as you feel. Exercise allows you to improve your body image; you can build muscle, lose pounds, gain

Kristen Murdoch

endurance, and be in the best physical shape of your life. Any form of exercise, whether it is running before work each morning or joining a gym, will have an effect on how you look in a positive way.

Exercise does not always have to be about the physical aspect, either. Each time you reach one of those goals, your morale and self confidence is raised up to a new level. If you are faced with a problem that may bring you down, you can think back to the ten extra push ups you were able to do before bed the night before, or the fifteen seconds faster you ran this morning. Peace of mind does not effect only you either; the better you feel about yourself, the better others will feel about you as well.

I am hoping you can now see exercise is a key to many doors. In my case, exercise was the key to finding something I was passionate about, and it really did change my life. I do not know where I would be today without my horseback riding and the benefits it has bestowed upon me. I am truly lucky and incredibly grateful to have found a form of exercise I enjoy so much, and that is so good for me.

I cannot urge you enough to get active and get involved in exercise. Whether you join a sports team or start running around your block, exercise will help you in so many ways. I cannot even begin to describe all of the doors that have been opened for me thanks to my discovery that, "exercise is key."

The enjoyment I get from exercise and the physical shape it leaves me in are enough incentive to continue as I have been. All forms of exercise are not for every person, as I found out first-hand. Trying new things and having an open mind will allow anyone to find something they can succeed at and benefit from.

There are so many ways to exercise, also. Even in your own home, you can exercise while watching television. During commercial breaks do a few sit-ups, see how many push ups you can do, do a couple of crunches each commercial! Your at-home exercise does not have to be as physically taxing, though. Stress-free exercise methods, such as yoga and Pilates are becoming more popular each day.

Exercise is something some people are born enjoying; others are not. If you are one of those people who is not born with this desire; however, all it takes is some searching. If a form of exercise can become fun, it can change your life. I know my life has been changed forever since I got involved with running and riding, and I can't imagine myself any other way. Exercise is a key that can open so many doors; don't let your doors remain locked.

Kristen Murdoch

# 10

# What Is an Athlete's Diet?

"The effects of steroids on girls results in a deep voice, irregular menstruation, and facial hair (Steroids). Facial hair, ladies! That is unacceptable! I don't care what kind of athlete I was, I would not risk getting a beard for anyone. And then the next thing you know kids in school will start calling me Wesley or some other boy name."

   To diet or not to diet?  Many teen athletes have asked themselves this question throughout the years.  But the truth is that there is no clear answer to this question.  It all depends on your body, type, genetics, and health.  Only you know what your body truly needs in order for you to have optimum performance.  No matter how many times someone tells you to do something, it is clear that as a teenager that you're probably going to do whatever you want anyway.  Nevertheless, before you make any decision as to whether dieting is the right path to take, it's best to get all of the facts first.

   The human body is very complex and delicate; too much strain on muscles and bones can cause a lot of damage, especially if you are undernourished.  Depriving your body of vital nutrients will only hinder your performance during a game or meet.  As an athlete, you need to take in more calories than your less active peers, according to a teen health article titled "A Guide to Eating for Sports."  Apparently, the extra calories are essential for optimum performance because daily exercise requires a lot of energy.  Therefore, since you are doing a lot more physical activity than your non athletic friends, it is normal for you to eat more food than them.

   Don't be scared if you feel as if you are gaining weight by taking in more calories.  It's a good thing because your body develops muscle mass faster than it does fat.  So you are actually doing your body a favor by eating more because now you will be able to have more stamina and more endurance.  If you don't believe me, then think back to a bad practice, game, or meet that you had recently or in the past.  Were you eating properly?  Did you eat enough in the days leading up to the event or the day of?  If you didn't then you probably didn't have a proper athletic diet.

   It is essential that your body gets the proper vitamins, nutrients, and minerals that it needs if you ever expect to become a top athlete or the best athlete that you can possibly be.  Training long hours every day will do little good if you are not eating properly to go along with it.  Teens these days seem

Wislande Guillaume

to have this outrageous belief that there is a quick way to improve performance. Well, I am here to tell you that there is no quick way to improve any kind of athletic performance.

Furthermore, a person's body type and genetics should be taken into account when trying to improve any kind of athletic performance. Say, for example, obesity runs in the family, you are several pounds overweight, and you want to try out for volleyball. It isn't practical to think that you could lose all that weight overnight, or even at all. In those situations, you would need to be practical and logical; because even if you did lose weight, there is no guarantee that you will ever be slim or muscular. On the other hand, a person who is already an athlete still faces the problem of genetics, so don't be alarmed if you are not losing weight at the same rate as your friends or fellow athletes. All body types are different. Moreover, even if you are not trying to lose weight, genetics will still be a factor. For example, many athletes spend hours training and working out to get large muscles. Sadly, some athletes are not able to obtain large muscles because their body makeup is just not built for large muscles. But don't be discouraged; anything is possible; just don't kill yourself over the problem or begin to use steroids, which will be discussed later.

All balanced diets require proper hydration. I can't stress enough how important hydration is in your performance. As an athlete myself, I have been known for not hydrating enough. The greatest harm you can do to your body is depriving it of water. When you sweat during your workout, you lose a lot of water, and if you do not replace the water lost, then you are just asking for injury. First of all, the lack of hydration causes your body to work harder than usual which puts more strain on your muscles, and you have to use more energy which could cause you to pull or strain a muscle. Worse yet, lack of hydration can cause you to lose consciousness which really won't get you anywhere. So you are better off drinking enough water so that you don't injure yourself. I bet now you're probably wondering how much hydration is needed for optimum performance. Experts recommend 1-2 cups of water before practice and hydrating every 15-20 minutes during practice ("A Guide to Eating for Sports"). For long distance runners, this can be kind of difficult, so it is best to drink plenty of water throughout the day, so that when practice comes, enough water is stored in the body. This will make running long distances a bit easier to manage. Finally, there has been enough talk about a lack of hydration, now it is time to discuss the things that are essential for a balanced diet.

First of all, carbohydrates are essential for optimum performance. I can't stress enough about how important a good intake of carbohydrates is. Carbohydrates are stored in the liver as glycogen. Basically, glycogen is liver sugar that the body uses to fuel the brain and muscles. Without enough glycogen in the body, athletes become fatigued and are not able to maximize their potential. This is effectively very important for people that are running long distances or play a sport that requires a lot of endurance. The carbohydrates allow you to become a faster, stronger, and an altogether more efficient athlete. Likewise, a diet high in carbohydrates allows the body to use fuel more efficiently because it does not have to work as hard as it would have to if there were not enough carbohydrates stored in the body. The body uses less glycogen during workouts which allows you to get more from your workout. Additionally, there are two types of carbohydrates that you can take, simple and complex carbohydrates. Simple carbohydrates include candy, sweets and sodas. In taking these kinds of carbohydrates would not be beneficial for optimal performance because they provide empty calories to the body. In contrast, complex carbohydrates are the best for the body. They are easily and quickly digested; as a result the body can obtain more energy quickly when needed. Foods that are excellent sources of complex carbohydrates are grains, cereals, bread, and starchy foods. Furthermore, the percentage of carbohydrates that is recommended for a balanced diet is 55-70% (Nutrients for Athletes).

Moreover, a good supply of protein, calcium and

Wislande Guillaume

88

minerals and fats are also essential to any athletic diet regimen. The protein allows the muscle to gain more muscle strength so that it can withstand strenuous activities such as playing football, soccer, and running. Although protein is important in a diet, too much protein can harm the body by causing dehydration, calcium loss, and other problems according to the article, "A Guide to Eating for Sports." Also, proteins are not as easily broken down by the body as carbohydrates are; therefore, the body utilizes a lot of energy to break down the protein (Nutrients for Athletes). Foods that are rich in protein include fish, eggs, lean red meat, and whole grains ("A Guide to Eating for Sports"). Likewise, calcium is essential for the building of strong bones. Not having enough calcium in the body can cause stress fractures ("A Guide to Eating for Sports"). Therefore, in order to get a good supply of calcium, you must eat foods that contain dairy products, such as yogurt or cheese or by drinking plenty of milk, approximately one glass a day. Additionally, fats are essential in workouts that are low in intensity and that require a lot of endurance. Because there is an abundance of fat in the body, more of it is utilized in these workouts than carbohydrates because there are limited amounts of it. Consequently, too much fat in the body is quite harmful to performance because it limits the amount of carbohydrates that can be stored in the body (Nutrients for Athletes).

It is now time to discuss the foods that are bad for you. Eating fast foods on a regular basis or drinking soda does nothing but harm your body. Fast foods are fatty and FULL OF CHOLESTEROL. Just think about the fat oozing out of that seemingly juicy double bacon cheeseburger. That same fat that is oozing out of it will slide right into your stomach to be processed by your body. Then all that fat will just travel throughout your body and just sit there. It's just a clogged artery waiting to happen. Just don't even go there. It is just not worth the risk. There are no positive benefits gained from eating them. I know that they taste good, but please refrain. It will be worth it in the long run. And, if you are going to eat fast foods or junk foods, do not eat them before a game or meet; it is just a disaster.  I remember one time freshman year in track, I decided to eat a bag of chips before I ran; it was one of the worst decisions that I could have possibly made.  I felt sharp stomach pains throughout the entire race.  And if any of you have experienced a similar event, you know exactly what I am talking about, but if you don't, that is good.

Furthermore, proper nutrition is not the only factor that is important in an athlete's diet; sleep is essential as well.  I bet I know what you're asking yourself right now.  Well, the answer is yes; going to bed late is detrimental to your performance.  Not getting enough sleep is horrendous for anyone, let alone an athlete!  It is probably one of the biggest mistakes that coaches point out to athletes all the time.  But I'm sure that you probably still do it all the time, and if you don't, I commend you.  Those of you that don't go to sleep early should start now and not wait.  It is hard enough to be an athlete; don't add more problems to yourself by getting to bed late because it does not do any good.  The worst part about it is that you're probably not doing anything useful when you're staying up late anyway.  It is not as if you were staying up doing your homework, a project or something else along those lines.  You're probably up talking on the phone, leaving comments on Myspace® or Facebook®, or just watching television.  This is one of the worst things that you can do; because if you keep staying up late, you will eventually screw up a performance that you would normally have excelled at as you don't have enough energy to concentrate on what you are doing.  Just don't do it to yourself.  Go to sleep early, so that you can be alert enough to practice well and have a good game or meet.  There is no sense in harming your body because it won't get you anywhere.

Finally, I'm sure that many of you have heard about the detrimental effects of steroids, but I am going to remind you anyway, just in case you are using them, thinking about using them, or even if you know someone that is using them.  First of all, there are a variety of reasons why athletes choose to use steroids. Some want to obtain larger muscles to increase performance because they can't accept that they their genes are preventing them from achieving the desired body type. Others might take steroids to become faster, more agile, or even more confident. But in all actuality, steroids will do you more harm than good. Even if you do obtain the desired body type, the effects on the body are excruciating. Taking steroids can result in liver tumors, jaundice, fluid retention, and high blood pressure. For males, it can result in testicular shrinkage, low sperm count, development of breasts, and baldness (Steroids). I don't know about you, but if I were a guy, I would be deathly afraid of shrinkage or growing boobs. Maybe my perspective is different from yours because I'm a girl, and my body is not the same as yours. I don't know as a guy, you might not mind the side effects, and if that is the case, then all the power to you.

But I'm sure that no teenage guy in their right mind would want shrinkage, baldness, or boobs. Can you say low-self esteem and social suicide? So please don't even do it to yourself. Likewise the same goes for girls, the effects of steroids on girls result in a deep voice, irregular menstruation, and facial hair (Steroids). Facial hair, ladies! That is unacceptable! I would not risk growing a beard for anyone. And then the next thing you know kids in school will start calling me Wesley or some other boy name. I don't think so, not in this lifetime. So please ladies, do even think about. If you ever want a guy to look twice at you, you had better think twice. No, better yet, don't even think about it. Just don't do it! Moreover, there are effects of steroids that affect both male and females, such as stunted growth and accelerated puberty. Accelerated puberty, are you kidding me? You're still in high school. It is illogical to think that the way you are in high school is the same way that you are going to be for the rest of your life.

You will change! Stop stressing about it. Never let anyone pressure you into taking steroids, and if you are currently taking steroids, STOP because if you get caught, you

What Is An Athlete's Diet?

are screwed.  SCREWED!!! Take your examples from the latest professional athletes who have gotten caught, such as Marion Jones, a track star, and Floyd Landis, the 2007 Tour de France champion.  Do not imitate their stupidity, as they ended up losers in the end.  Maybe you don't care about becoming a professional athlete in the grand scheme of things, and you just want to take steroids in high school, so you can get into a top school and play in college.  Before I go any further, think about the potential scholarships that could be lost if you get caught.  Just think about the potential consequences of your actions.  Love yourself enough to not take the risk.

In the end, it is clear to see that many factors contribute to a balanced athletic diet.  Eating properly, exercising efficiently, are all key components that will allow you to maximize your potential to be a tremendous athlete.  In any case, I would entreat all athletes and future athletes to take control of your lives and do what is best for your lives.  As a teenager, these are the pivotal moments in your life that are shaping the person that you will eventually become.  Treat yourself well, and don't take steroids.  Don't risk your future and health.  Do the right thing.  Take these tips that I have given you, and try to apply it to your current diet, you won't regret it.  For more information about the information listed visit www.teenhealthandwellness.com.

Wislande Guillaume

# 11

# Watch Out For the *Big Girls*?!

"Learn to separate your physical body from your identity"

Have you been feeling down lately? Have others recently commented on your outside appearance? Have you ever felt like wrapping yourself up in thousands of blankets and hiding from the eyes of the public? Do you feel like you are carrying around extra baggage? Well... you are definitely not the only one in the world who feels that everyone is carefully observing the way you eat, talk, walk, and sleep. You are just simply paranoid.

Obesity is at an all time high! Surprisingly enough, popular public opinion has never been so obsessed with being thin. I would have thought that by now, everyone would have learned to appreciate their own body and treat it as if it was their own temple. If you feel upset about being overweight, you should not make it obvious to the public. It is easy to stare at other women who are thin and men that are muscular, to avoid our own problems with our personal weight. Instead of trying to avoid your own problems, do something about it! Establish healthy diets or simply work with what your momma gave you!

In today's society, it is always difficult to find someone who is completely satisfied with their body weight and shape. Everyone carries along with them a distorted image of their own body. Just because you carry around an embarrassing picture of yourself does not mean the entire world feels the same way. What is your primary motivation to lose weight? Why can't you just be happy with the way you are? Why are you putting yourself through the trouble of obtaining the so-called "ideal body weight"?

Dieting is obviously the most common way that people today tend to use in order to improve on their public image. There are plenty of other methods that can also be helpful in mentally enhancing your body image. Several individuals have become so adapted to our culture that they assume that their physical identity defines who they are. Physical appearance is, by no means whatsoever, enmeshed with your identity and who you are as an individual. Remember... you can never judge a book by its cover. Similarly, you can never assume an

Reshma Niyamathullah

individual's personality just by looking at his or her physical appearance. You have to realize that you are more than just a body. Learn to separate your physical body from your identity. What appears to be your body from the outside will never come anywhere close to how you feel in the inside.

Believe in yourself as a unique individual by believing in your body. The only way to reach a pure state of happiness is if you allow yourself to clear your mind of unnecessary thoughts. Do not make yourself feel overweight. Be proud of who you are and what you look like. Use your body to your advantage. Use your body to boost your self-confidence. Being skinny is not going to make you completely content with yourself and with your life. You need to be truly satisfied with your inner being in order to reach the highest level of contentment. Only you have the authority to choose to be happy... whether you are overweight or not.

Never let the opinions of others become enmeshed into your own mind. What others think is not what you think, which is why you must learn to choose your friends wisely. Some individuals in society have a tendency to become obsessed with the way they look. Learn to carefully choose friends who accept you for who you are, not for what size you are. Never let others take advantage of you by humiliating you and your overweight body. Use your body to your own advantage! Never let others control the way you feel. Never let others have any impact on your thoughts. Be your own individual... be you.

The popular media is obsessed with looks more than you will ever be in your entire lifetime. Because the media promotes physical appearance as the most important feature of individuals living in society, viewers are convinced that they are not perfect individuals because they do not have the "ideal body" or the "perfect look." The advertising industry is based upon one prominent idea: they are only interested in making you feel as if there is something wrong with you mentally or physically in order to persuade you to buy their products. Never let the advertising industry gain control of your body!

Watch Out For the *Big Girls*?!

For those individuals who find it difficult to reach high levels of confidence and greater levels of self-esteem mentally, a healthy diet can always enhance your physical features, which, in turn, will enable you to appreciate your body to a greater extent. A healthy diet starts with exercise. Without a healthy diet plan, it would be difficult and impossible to maintain a certain weight loss over a long period of time. Exercise is the fundamental basis of any healthy diet. By simply exercising a few times a week for at least twenty minutes each day, you can easily be guaranteed a decent amount of weight loss without becoming anorexic or bulimic!

It is true that fat loss is about calorie reduction. However, a calorie intake which is incredibly low, can seriously harm your body and more significantly, damage your health. Never let a diet become a threat to your body. Never let a diet become a threat to your health. Most importantly, never let a diet become a threat to your life! By saying, "I'm not going to eat because I need to lose weight!" is absolutely ridiculous. What some individuals do not realize is that starving your body of certain foods will not allow you to lose a good amount of weight in the long run. The only effects would be growing feelings of irritation, fatigue, and weak muscles. It is likely that you will begin to binge or even return to your normal eating habits, which will cause you to gain additional weight. Dieting in a healthy manner is always important!

A typical weight loss program aims for a loss of one to two pounds each week. In order to prevent subsequent weight gain and loss of muscle, only individuals that are truly overweight should concentrate on losing more than one to two pounds each week. There are several programs that encourage and promote a nutritional balance while providing low calories. Because some of these programs can result in a daily calorie intake of less than eight hundred calories, such rapid weight loss programs are always most effective if supervised by an individual with authority, experience, and knowledge.

There are several risks to rapid weight loss programs. If there is no supervision, nutritional deficiencies can result,

Reshma Niyamathullah

which, in turn, will lead to potential health problems. A lack of fiber will also lead to problems such as constipation, irritability, and fatigue. A lowered metabolism can even possibly begin an unhealthy pattern of yo-yo dieting. What is most undesirable is a loss of muscle mass, known as catabolism, as well as fat. Because of these possible health deficiencies, rapid weight loss programs are encouraged only for individuals who are truly obese, not for the skinny girls who all of a sudden became "fat" overnight because somebody told them that they are looking a little chunky...

I remember when I was younger, my brothers and I would always make random jokes about my cousin because she was overweight when she was only in elementary school. My brothers would never stop with the jokes until they could see the tears rushing down her face. It seemed funny at the time, but if you saw my cousin now, your jaw would probably drop (and nobody would be there to pick it up for you)! The non-stop fat jokes obviously got to her head. I remember we always used to tell her that she was so fat that her friends had to grease the door frame and hold a Twinkie® on the other side just to get her through! Despite all the criticism, she gradually learned to accept herself for who she is, not for what she looks like. As the years progressed, she followed healthy diets and exercised on a daily basis. She realized that the more secure she is about her body, the less criticism she heard from others. After realizing that she needs to appreciate her body, she was working on her personality, inside and out!

Look at Mo'Nique. She is a living example of a proud, overweight, beautiful woman, actress, television host, and comedian. She is letting the entire world know that no matter what they say about the big girls, nobody can ever tear them into pieces. Mo'Nique has what a lot of other beautiful, skinny women lack – self-respect, appreciation, admiration, and love for her body. By making all her extra baggage look sexy, she is inspiring overweight women to accept their inner beauty.

If you ask anyone who has been struggling to achieve a healthy body weight, I guarantee you that they will stress about

Watch Out For the *Big Girls*?!

how it is not an easy thing to do. Why is losing weight so hard? Well... the answer is very simple. There is a huge difference between knowing *what* to do and *actually doing it*. Reading about how to lose weight is not going to make you ten pounds lighter by the end of the week. Sorry to kill the dreams of any aspiring magicians out there, but no magic pill exists to all of a sudden reduce your weight! It takes time, hard work, and persistence to achieve your ideal body weight. Live in a healthy way emotionally, physically, and spiritually. Take care of your health by maintaining an appropriate diet, but always remember to love yourself for who you are inside and out.

Reshma Niyamathullah

# 12

# What's the Skinny?

"...learn to love yourself for what is inside and not what you see in the mirror, because your looks will not always be the same, but the heart is genuine and your inner beauty can last forever."

Why do people diet?  Why is everyone obsessed with weight?  Why is it a social trend to be super-skinny?  The "skinny race," as I prefer to call it, has led many girls down a detrimental road.  No one should want to travel this road, but while dieting you can be lead the wrong way, and you might just end up at a dead end (literally and metaphorically).  A dead end!  If you are dieting or thinking about dieting, you should certainly make sure you are traveling down the right path.  Dieting is not a joke.  Many times people rashly decide to diet, and they do not know how to do diet correctly.  Dieting should not be taken lightly.  When should you diet?  What is a healthy weight?  How do you know if you have taken it too far?  When does dieting become an eating disorder?

Most teenagers, especially girls, are overly concerned about their weight.  Before going on a diet ask yourself, "Am I at a healthy weight?"  It may be hard to answer this question by yourself, especially if you are already disillusioned about dieting.  Before anyone goes on a diet, it would be wise to ask your doctor what your Body Mass Index (BMI) is, and get his or her opinion on whether or not you should go on a diet.  This can help you significantly.  If your BMI is normal, why go on a diet?  Some people cannot use this logic.  As a teenager, you must remember that you are at a crucial stage of your growth and development, and weight gain is a part of it.  So why do people have eating disorders?

Pressure from the media, friends, parents, and other environmental influences have engraved the idea of being super-slim into the minds of young people.  This causes people to have a distorted body image.  Distorted body image is a leading cause of eating disorders.  In order to visualize what a distorted body image would be like, imagine that a perfectly normal girl is looking into a funhouse mirror.  This girl does not see her typical self; instead, she sees a girl with a fat body.  If you feel like you are looking in a funhouse mirror when you are looking in a regular mirror, this may be a warning for the onset of an eating disorder or distorted body image.  Situations like this, along with other factors, encourage people suffering from

Kadeisha Kilgore

eating disorders to either move on or get worse.

An obsession with a diet that is bound to fail can be a prelude to any of the three major types of eating disorders. The three major eating disorders are: anorexia nervosa, bulimia nervosa, and binge eating disorder. Eating disorders are life-threatening; they not only affect the person who has one, but the lives of their loved, ones too. Living with an eating disorder is painful, physically and emotionally. The effects, both short and long term, are really numerous. As a result of suffering from an eating disorder, there are social problems, health problems, and physical problems.

Anorexia is self-imposed starvation. This mental illness causes severe physical problems. Anorexia has one of the highest mortality rates of any mental illness. The root of the disorder is typically emotional issues. Young women, between the ages of fifteen and twenty-four, have a twelve times greater chance of dying at a young age than their friends do. The physical problems associated with this disorder include: esophageal rupture, heart failure, and stroke. Many people fail to realize that anorexia affects all ages, genders, and ethnic backgrounds.

Bulimia is a mental disorder, in which a person overeats and then purges. Bulimia can be a deadly cycle. Purging is not just vomiting; it can be done using laxatives, diuretics, or even exercising excessively. A person with bulimia often feels helpless, depressed, or anxious. Bulimia is a sign that someone has lost control, but those who are suffering from it sometimes do so as an attempt to gain some control in life. By no means is bulimia a single-gender eating disorder. Researchers find one male with bulimia for every ten to fifteen females.

Binge eating disorder is the newest clinically recognized eating disorder. BED is characterized by repeated episodes of uncontrolled eating. People suffering from this generally do not stop eating until they are uncomfortably full. Nonetheless, BED is not associated with behaviors, such as vomiting or excessive exercise, to rid the body of extra food. The illness is found in more women than men, but overall, researchers have found that it is the most common eating disorder. Overeating in individuals with BED often leads to feeling out of control and feelings of depression, guilt, or disgust. The medical problems associated with this disorder are similar to those found in obesity.

Ask yourselves these questions, to see where you stand on the perception of body image. The scenario is that there are three high school sophomores, who are all very good friends but have no similarities in body image. Jenny is 90 pounds and tall; is she overweight, underweight or just right? Mia is 123 pounds and tall; is she overweight, underweight, or just right? Jaslene is 225 pounds and short; is she overweight, underweight, or just right? How you will answer these questions can say a lot about you. By no means is this a diagnostic test; it is just a way to compare people's perceptions. The way different people perceive things varies from one person to the next. A normal person would say that Jenny is underweight, Mia is just right, and Jaslene is overweight. Does everyone answer this way? No. For those of you who think Jenny is just right, you need to pay close attention to the detrimental effects associated with people like Jenny.

It is amazing how we perceive things as humans since we are all so very different from each other. On the "Tyra Banks" show, she did a social experiment on people of different ethnic backgrounds. She placed different people behind a curtain and asked a representative of each ethnic group what they thought about the subject's size. A number of people perceived an extremely skinny person as someone who looked healthy. I was shocked that so many people perceived the woman as someone healthy, because she looked like she was dying of starvation. It is really sad that people think skinny equals happy, pretty, and all the best things in the world.

If you are suffering from an eating disorder, get help! It does not make you an extremely bad person for having an

Kadeisha Kilgore

eating disorder, but it does make you a better person if you seek help. Realizing that you need help is the first step to getting better. It will not be easy, but it is certainly the best thing to do. What you must remember is that things are going to get easier and that you are going to get healthier.

If you know a friend who is suffering from an eating disorder, reach out to him or her. It is nice to have someone to lean on when you are not strong. Helping others is essential, because one day you might need help. It is very important not to ignore a friend or her problem, if you think she has an eating disorder. Ignoring an eating disorder does not solve the problem. So try to be supportive to a friend. If your friend does not want to listen to you, and you love that friend, then it would be wise to tell their parents or another adult that could help. I know you are probably thinking, "I don't wanna rat out my friends," but in this case, if you do not tell someone about your friend, you may no longer have them. You should not view the situation as "ratting a friend out;" instead, you should believe that you are helping your friend the best way that you know how to. In the long run, you could be saving a life. My point is, seek advice for your friend out of love, and later, they will love you even more for doing it.

If you are recovering from an eating disorder, give other people hope. It is good encouragement to others, who are suffering, to see someone who was once like them, back in control of their lives in a healthy manner. It is a great accomplishment to be recovering from an eating disorder, because it is just as hard as being addicted to drugs and having to go to rehab.

Something that everyone must stop doing is believing the media. The media is the main reason why people turn to dieting and why people develop eating disorders. It is popular belief that skinny is "in". If you ask me, being super-skinny is not cute. Super-skinny people look like skeletons with skin on them. I am skinny, (not super-skinny), and it is not "pie in the sky". As a child, everyone called me names like, "Skinny Minnie", "Stix", "Bones", and "Legs"(because they're so long and thin). Sometimes I would get mad, but I never became obsessed with my weight. I do not want to be fat, but I do not want to be super-skinny. Why? Because I love the skin that I am in; it's the way God made me, and I am proud of it. You should be too. Embrace your body, and learn to love yourself; because if you don't, no one else will. Once I learned to stop retaliating when people said, "You are so skinny," they stopped bothering me. I would say, "I don't care; I like being small, and I am not that skinny." Yes, I am small, but I have a healthy weight for my age. So do not let dieting push you to an extreme. Do not diet to the point where you look so thin that it is sickening, because there is nothing pretty about it.

Consider the fact that the modeling industry is now accepting more and more plus-sized models. Also, if you are too skinny, they do not want you to represent their agency. Previously the modeling industry would only want super-thin girls, but after the surge of models dying from eating disorders, they ended their search for super-thin girls. Do not kill yourself in the race to be super-skinny.

Dieting is not always right for everybody. If it leads to the point where you develop an eating disorder, it definitely is not right. Stop worrying about what other people think of you, because it only matters what you think of you. It is not horrible to diet, but if you do not need to, then what is the point? Know your limitations, and seek advice when you do not know them. Eat healthy foods, and take care of the body that you have. Most importantly, learn to love yourself for what is inside and not what you see in the mirror, because your looks will not always be the same, but your inner beauty can last forever.

Kadeisha Kilgore

# 13

# Relationships: Isn't It Funny the Way Things Work Out?

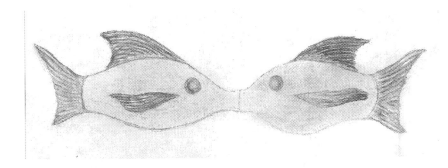

"It's not the things that were said, but the things that weren't said. I liked the smell of his ugly jacket, and the way our history teacher would have to watch us when he played a movie, just to make sure we weren't doing anything sixth graders weren't supposed to be doing."

In your lifetime, you will go through many different types of relationships. As a child, you may have thought that the only relationships that existed were those between yourself and a significant other. However, if you're probably like me, you're at that point in your life where you realize that there is more to life than the whole boyfriend and girlfriend relationship. There are many different kinds of relationships, including professional ones, acquaintances, family relationships, abusive connections, friends, and other intimates, just to name a few. The ways we interact with people make us who we are today and affect us in the future. In this chapter, you will learn more about the different kinds of relationships and how some of my experiences can help you in the future.

## Professional Relationships

When I was younger, I found myself saying that I would never get a job when I was in high school. However, as you grow up, you may find yourselves needing things that you don't really want your parents to pay for. In my experience as a student/worker, it is sometimes difficult to be myself, while not crossing the line of being unprofessional.

I got my first job as a tutor. Being professional with my bosses was no problem, because they were laid back and understood that I was still a teenager in high school, and that sometimes it was difficult to maintain both a job and good grades. At times, you may encounter people that are not as nice as my first boss. It is important to know where you stand with a person. You should not cross the line where you make things awkward where you put yourself and that person in an uncomfortable position. You need to respect each other in all situations.

My boss was easy to deal with, the kids-not so much. When you are surrounded by a bunch of children under the age of fourteen for four straight hours, it may be difficult to function. Even when the kids would cross the line, I found it

Jessica Samson

difficult to not make a joke at them at their expense. As someone older and wiser, I had to make it clear to that I was the authority; I needed to be a role model for these kids.

You shouldn't act this way just with kids though; you should act this way with everyone. When I got my second job, I worked at a restaurant where you had to interact with people all day. Most people are nice, and you have to be professional with them, letting them know that you are doing your job correctly and meeting up to their standards. There are certain types of common courtesy rules that need to be followed, whether you see the person the next week or never again. However, there are always those people that are going to get on your nerves, and if put in a difficult situation, you would want to say something to them. In these situations, you need to just think about what you are going to do, and figure out if it's worth it in the long run. There's a great quote from the book, A Separate Peace, where author John Knowles says, "You have to do the right thing, but make sure it's the right thing in the long run and not just for the moment." In dealing with professional relationships with people, you don't have to be best friends with everyone, but you do have to try and make the best of what you can with them.

A professional relationship that many of you can relate to is the ones between you and your teachers. You don't have to like your teachers, but you should respect them, not just to get a good grade. Developing a professional relationship with your teacher eventually helps you in your studies in the future when you need help with your school work. These professional relationships you build through the years make you grow as a person. Think about it; teachers are the one giving you information, so if you want to collaborate with your teacher in some way you need to first develop a professional relationship with them.

## Acquaintances

Acquaintances are those people that you talk to, but you might never hang out with in real life as a friend. This is a normal thing, and you shouldn't be fazed over the fact that this may be all that your relationship with that person amounts to. Acquaintances keep us interacting with people; in a way, they keep us sane. Acquaintances have their many good aspects because they help us with the little things. It's human nature to need help, and by developing uncomplicated relationships with people, you allow yourself more opportunities to get help in unfamiliar situations. Through these acquaintances, you might develop friendships.

## Family

There are many relationships in your family, and each one is different. There may be the uncle you don't like or your favorite cousin, but no matter what, you still have a different relationship with each of them. Family relationships are the first ones we learn about when we are little kids. These are the ones that shape us into the person we grow up to be. Family relationships are the most important. Because of them, we can become a healthier, more stable person. Good family relationships help us to communicate with others.

Being a girl, it is stereotypical to become "Daddy's Little Girl;" this was never the case with me. Although I am okay with my father now, I grew up in fear of him. My dad used to have a temper, and I remember instances when he would just take it out on the world. The littlest thing would set him off, and I remember hiding from him, as he tore apart our house. I remember going downstairs to find my mother in tears, with plates broken, the furniture in an upheaval, and one time, the trophies he had won, lay broken. I'm sure everyone's family fights a lot, but there were times when I felt my dad loved his cars, which he spent more than half his time with, than me, his own daughter. There were even periods

Jessica Samson

of time where he didn't come home for a while, and I'd get mad at him. There are times when you question your family if they still love you anymore. Yes. They're supposed to, but it didn't seem like it when my dad woke me up in the middle of the night as an eight year old, telling me to search for his passport because he was going to leave.

I don't want you to think my dad is a bad person, because he's not. He provides for his family, even if he is stubborn at times. I've seen a change in him through the years, and if I ever did build upon my relationship with him, I'd tell him that. However, I hope someday I will, but as for right now, it's stuck in the teenage stage where I'm comfortable where I am with him and don't want to make things awkward.

My mom's amazing and has always been there for me. Mothers are the ones that will love you no matter what. They are our natural nurturers. Our relationships with our mothers have always been there, even before birth.

If you're like me, you have a sibling. I have one sister who is two years younger than me. When we were younger, we used to get in fights all the time, but as I have gotten older, our relationship has gotten closer. Although her words can be bitter and leave a nasty mark on my heart, I know she will always look out for me and be there. Blood is thicker than water, and no matter what grudges you may hold against a sibling or any other member of your family, you need to learn how to be the bigger man and expand your relationship.

I'm the oldest on both sides, meaning I am the oldest sister, cousin, and grandchild. It's a lot of pressure to be put under this situation because I know I have more than a dozen cousins looking at me on how to live their lives. I want to make my family happy, so they need an example for their children. It is for my cousins that I make myself be a better person, so they can follow the example.

Relationships: Isn't It Funny the Way Things Work Out?

<u>Friends, Boyfriends, and Abusive Relationships</u>

Everyone needs a friend in life. Throughout your life you're going to go through many different friends in your life; some of them may be friends for many years, and others can be fake. You need to learn in life the difference between the two, so you can develop relationships with the ones that matter. Your friends are the ones that will always be there for you and the ones that you can count on.

I have been through dozens of friends. It's not because I'm not a good person or anything, but things just change throughout the years. The interests in elementary, middle, and high school all differ and require different people to back you up in what you are doing. It may seem kind of ironic that friends and abusive relationships can be in the same category, but sometimes the people that can be considered your best friends, are the ones that can be taken for granted and become the most abusive.

When I was in fourth grade, I had two best friends. Now, I wasn't the skinniest of kids and looking back at it now, I probably ate more than I do now, (which is saying a lot), but they liked me for who I was, or so I thought. I was the kind of kid that raised my hand to answer a question whenever I knew an answer, and the one that asked the teacher if they ever needed anything. It's sad to say that even in fourth grade, you can still give into peer pressure. After talking to them, they asked me why I raised my hand so much and even called me names, like teacher's pet. I slowly stopped raising my hand as much, and the teachers started giving me funny looks, but I didn't care; I just wanted my friends to like me.

Then, towards the end of fourth grade, my friends just stopped talking to me. At recess, I tried to confront them and ask them why they weren't talking to me. I would run after them and ask them, "What do I have to do to get you to talk to me?" They would reply, "Nothing." I would stand frozen like in freeze tag, and moments later say, "Well, see? Aren't I doing what you want?" They would snicker and laugh at me and say,

Jessica Samson

"Well, you're breathing. Go away." They would run off, and I would continue to follow them like a dog on a leash.

This went on for a week, until my longest and truest best friend, Alyssa, asked me why I kept following them. I thought she didn't understand. I needed them. They were our close friends, too! How could they just stop talking to me? Then she told me what they had said and had told her, "We don't want to be friends with that fat loser anymore."

I was crushed. These were my best friends. Even in fourth grade, you can still be hurt. Sure, sticks and stones I understand, but these words were scarring. These aren't the kind of words you learn from a private school. I began to find a new group of friends that I knew wouldn't say anything, but I could never really get close to them. Yet, the same group of "friends" I had continued to taunt me and whispered, as I tried to play dodge ball in the playground.

At the end of fourth grade, it was announced that I was going to Central Five. One of the girls I hadn't talked to since the incident turned to me and said, "But I thought you said you were going to graduate from here? You said you'd be here all the way to eighth grade." "Yeah. Right." I was going to stay here another four years, so you could continue to taunt and make fun of me. We were on the line to go to lunch, and she was right in front of me and had not noticed that the line was leaving her. Even though it wasn't very nice, I looked at her and said, "Well, I'm not." I gave her the dirtiest look a fourth grader could give someone and walked past her to lunch, leaving her and the rest of pained memories of them behind me.

Public school turned out to be even better than I expected it to be. However, as we get older, we naturally get attracted to the opposite sex. My first "boyfriend" was in sixth grade. He was this cute Portuguese kid that knew how to make me laugh. I never really paid attention to him, but my best friend Alyssa had a crush on him in fifth grade, and we all know how that goes: friend goes for friend's ex-crush. I know some may think that sixth grade is too young to like or actually love someone, but to this day, I ponder what feelings I had for

Relationships: Isn't It Funny the Way Things Work Out?

him. He wore this stupid black jacket with a red stripe, and everyone used to make fun of us, wondering if our braces got stuck when we kissed.

In any case, you could consider him my first love. It's not the things that were said, but the things that weren't said. I liked the smell of his ugly jacket and the way our history teacher would have to watch us when he played a movie, just to make sure we weren't doing anything sixth graders weren't supposed to be doing. The relationship didn't even last that long to be considered a relationship, but I would think about him almost everyday.

We ended on a bad note. There was another girl; let's call her Letasha, for confidentiality's sake. Letasha had claimed that she had been going out with him first and wondered who the hell I was. It's that middle school drama that gets to you. Alyssa and my best guy friends, Stephen and Nick, had told me many times to dump him, because he was lying, and they had seen him with Letasha numerous times. I confronted this guy, but he automatically denied it and said, "Stephen's a lying fruit cup, I love you only."

Love is so blind. On June 18, 2002, he walked into the auditorium with Letasha right next to him. My friends gasped at the sight, and I couldn't bear to look at him. They killed him with death looks, and I felt my heart breaking inside. By accident, I looked at him; her hand was in his, and he looked at me desperately, like I was supposed to save him or something. The bell rang, and I ran away from him before he could get the chance to say anything to me.

You don't have to know how I took the situation (I wrote a note to him saying it was over, and his music teacher read it out the whole class), what became of the two of them (they went out in the beginning of seventh grade), and what happened between her and me (she sat right next to me in my first period class the next year). However, it's funny the way things work out. They broke up. He started liking me again, but I never was one to make the same mistake twice. I've liked

Jessica Samson

him on and off for six years now. I even wrote a note to him in eighth grade, saying he could come to me if he ever needed anything. Even as a graduating senior, I wonder how he grew up and if he's happy. I wonder if he ever thinks about me, and I still wonder if he'd call me years from now, wondering how I am.

It's because of this one event in my life that has caused me to have trust issues with any other guy that has ever tried to get close to me, or I have tried to get close to. Throughout my life, there have been boys that liked me that I wasn't really into, or guys that I knew I could never get with. It's just safer that way. If a guy had a girlfriend or I never talked to him, then I would never be an option for him and therefore, would never get hurt. I had my close friends, and that's what I tried to convince myself all that I needed to make me happy.

During my sophomore year, I had a cotillion, one of those fancy dances that goes along with a Sweet Sixteen. In a nutshell, seventeen of my friends and I would gather together almost every weekend for five months learning how to salsa and waltz. I had already come to terms with who my best friends were, and we all called ourselves the "BEASTS", each one of us standing for a letter (I was the B, because I was considered the "boss" of the group). In any case, the guy I liked was in my cotillion, but he had a girlfriend, so I considered myself safe. Still, the temptation was still there, and it can be awfully hard to repress your feelings for a guy when you're always around him.

Things began to grow shaky in the last few weeks before my party, because the "E" in the BEASTS had gotten a boyfriend. She was in two cotillions at the same time, and her boyfriend happened to be in the other one. I started to get mad at her because she continued to miss practice after practice, affecting the timing and positions of the couples around us. She wouldn't even call me anymore and would make excuses about going to the other cotillion, when I needed her as well. For example, I had a practice, and she told me she had to leave early to go to a dentist appointment. I got kind of skeptical when another Kevin, who was in both cotillions as well, said he was going to the dentist as well. I had heard earlier in the day that the other cotillion was going to hang out in the center of our town, but weren't even practicing for anything. The other cotillion had ended already, and it was less than a week until my party.

I know it sounds kind of conceited about my talking about my party, but this just wasn't just important to me, it was important to my parents, family, and my friends. I really didn't even want a party in the first place, but my aunt had pushed me to have one, and I just wanted to please everyone. I wanted everything to be perfect, and it didn't help that she was starting to put her boyfriend before her best friends. I was there for her in everything, and I just couldn't understand why she had started to grow so shady and was drifting away.

So, she and Kevin ended up going to the "dentist." She lied straight to my face and said, "My mom's making me go; I'll try and come back later." As soon as she left, I yelled and vented to the rest of BEASTS. It wasn't that she wasn't going to practice and barely knew the dance and was missing practice; it was the fact that she could stand right in front of me and lie to my face like that. I knew where she was going; everyone in that whole room knew where she was going, and yet, she still had the nerve to lie to ME, one of her BEST friends. I was done with her, but my party was still a week away.

Our friendship was on its last straw, and it didn't help what she did on the day of the party. The Friday night before, she had partied with the other cotillion and was nowhere to be found the morning of my party. She was the first one on the list to get her hair done, and as the minutes passed by, I grew frantic. I had to call all the other girls to come earlier because of her irresponsibility. When she finally did show up, a good three hours later, I couldn't even look at her. It felt like she had stabbed me in the back. First, she lies to me; second, she can't even be there on the very rare occasions that I do actually need her. The whole schedule got messed up, and I ended up getting into a fight with my parents before the party started.

Jessica Samson

My mom needed my dad to give me a ride to the place, so I could take pictures and set up, but my dad couldn't understand why. My mom needed to get ready, and because we were running late, things weren't going as smoothly. I remember my dad on the phone, and the way he drove furiously down the highway. He got mad at me for having the party and even said he wasn't going to go.

I turned away toward my window, mascara flowing down my powdered face. How could my dad not even show up to my own Sweet Sixteen? Who was I supposed to dance with for the Father and Daughter dance?

As I said before, it's funny the way things work out. My party ended up amazing; my dad did finally show up, but "E" and I still aren't talking. I tried talking to her; I really did, but her excuse for not working things out is that she's "scared." I have learned that you have to be forgiving towards people that have hurt you, but what can you do when they're not even bothering to make an effort to try? I'm happy now, and I hope she finds happiness, too.

Abusive relationships vary in form. They can be the kind when you physically abuse someone or the kind where you mentally toil with someone. I have never experienced the first kind; however, I have learned that you can get help when you are going through something like this. You're only a victim if you choose to be a victim. There are many kinds of treatments out there, and you have many different relationships like friends and family to help you get through with these. However, I have experienced the second kind.

The same kid I liked in my cotillion; let's call him Michael, began having problems with his girlfriend; let's call her Ursula. I had grown close to Michael after my party, not because I liked him, because I didn't anymore, but because I felt sorry for the life he was living. He lived in an abusive home and didn't have a good relationship with his dad, and I felt like I could help him escape from all that. We hung out a few times, and I was the person he could talk to late at night in the summer or take a walk with when times were getting tough.

We had "our spot" in my house where we would just talk about all the problems we had. Meanwhile, the "A" in BEASTS had started to grow close to Michael as well, a little too close.

Following the tradition of silly high school drama, Ursula began to grow mad at "A," because she threatened her. To make a long story short, Ursula and Michael broke up, and Michael asked "A" out at our homecoming.

The moment "A" told me, I had a bad feeling. You know those bad feelings you get when you know this isn't a good thing? I got that when she told me. I couldn't dare to tell her though; she was so happy, and she was my best friend; I had to be happy for her. Still, there was that feeling inside me that told me something bad wasn't going to come out of this.

Junior year is always one of the hardest years, and there was a point in my life where I couldn't take it anymore. I would walk down the hallways of my high school feeling unhappy, and every time I saw Michael and "A" together, the pit in my stomach grew deeper and deeper. I didn't want to admit it at first, but I knew in the back of my head what was going on: I had started to like my best friend's boyfriend.

I had always been there for Michael, and I needed someone to talk to. If I had talked to my girlfriends, they would have told me to stop and to not mess everything up for everyone. Michael was someone I could trust, even if our relationship was going to be shaky after what I was going to tell him. Since he got kicked out of his dad's house, he lived with his brother and got much closer to me. Before I called him, I did one of those little bets with God like, "God, if he answers in less than two rings, then I'll go, but if it takes him more than one, I won't." Turns out, he picked up as soon as it rang.

I remember our taking a walk. I found myself turning around a couple of times but still found him at the doorway of the house. He looked at me, and I couldn't bear to look at him. I found myself turning towards a wall pouring out my heart to him. I told him about the problems at home. I told him about

Jessica Samson

this girl that threatened me because she thought I was spreading rumors about her. I told him how my heart hurt every time I had to see him and "A" in the hallways. I hated that I had sprained my ankle a few weeks before and felt so helpless sometimes. I couldn't take it that I had to pretend to be happy for everyone all the time.

He was at a loss for words, and all he could do was hug me as I cried into his arms.

Things started to grow less tense after I told him what had happened. In the midst of all this, we were planning a surprise dance for "A"s Sweet Sixteen, and Michael was in it. We had to practice for her affair that weekend, so we ended up seeing each other a lot.

On a cold, December night, my friend Chelsea and I had decided to kidnap people. We were having the time of our lives, just driving around and blasting music, until we decided to stop by Michael's house. Michael hopped in the car, and after watching a lame movie, Chelsea decided to drop us both off at my house. My parent's were both downstairs, so we went up to my room to watch TV.

I laid down on my bed, and it took a while for me to realize Michael was lying down next to me. We both turned on our sides toward the television, and I could feel his arms wrapped around me. His fingers were entwined with mine, as his face pushed itself into my hair. His feet were cold as they brushed mine, and it was one of those instances in your life where something feels so good and so bad at the same time. It was like everything was alright, until he mentioned "A"'s name, and I knew I wasn't into this. I got up, and told him it was getting late. He left, but I kept replaying everything that had just happened. This was my best friend's boyfriend. He knew how I felt about him, so why was he playing these mind games? I then received a message from him that said he needed to tell me something on Friday.

It seemed like forever until Friday came. We had practice for "A"'s surprise thing beforehand, so afterwards, he came back to my house. I asked him what he needed to tell me, but he just kept avoiding the question, as the minutes on the clock continued to pass by. He begged me to talk to him, as I continued to grow "mad" at him. Then in the end, he turned to me and looked at me: "Jess, I know you may only like me, but I don't know how to say this." I almost couldn't breathe as his brown eyes stared at me. "I love you."

My heart stopped. I hadn't heard those words in forever, but it was all confusion to me at the same time. I'm sure he hadn't said these words to "A" yet because she would have told me something. This was so wrong on so many levels. "And I just want to know how you feel back."

He looked at me there, hurt when I had said nothing. He was flipping the channels on my television as a distraction, but as he turned, he landed on a commercial that said, "I love you." I told him, "There's your answer." He looked at me and just smiled.

In the next weekend, I found myself getting closer to him, where we would rush practices just so we could be together at my house. However, there came a point in my life where I had told Alyssa what had happened, and she told me to end it quickly. I knew I couldn't do it anymore, so as I finished talking to her, I saw Michael walking and ran to catch up with him. I told him "A" was my best friend and that I couldn't do this to her. He looked crushed and called himself bad luck. After this happened, we tried to avoid each other and stayed away as much as we could, only giving the occasional head nod when our eyes did meet.

However at "A"'s party, everything changed. The party was great; it was the chain of events afterward that had me confused and all out of focus. After the party, Michael had texted me and said that I looked beautiful. I tried to think of it as nothing, but it seemed like he was starting to start something between us again.

On a weekend in January, my parents were going to Canada to visit my cousins. I didn't go because I had a Sweet Sixteen to go to that weekend. So I, the helplessly in love teenager I thought I was, invited Michael to spend the night. I

Jessica Samson

118

didn't do anything, but I liked him there beside me. It was tough sleeping next to him because I was so aware of everything that was going on inside of me. I felt shivers go up and down my spine like an elevator. He smelled like fresh soap, and he was so warm, despite the cold weather outside. We just hung out the whole day; I made breakfast, and he said things like, "so this is what the future is going to be like." He listened to the soccer game, while I fell asleep next to him. Then I started to get ready for the party. I shaved, put on some shorts and a t-shirt and went into my room to straighten my hair. As I continued straightening, he stared at me, and I asked what he was staring at. He said, "What? I'm not allowed to stare at something beautiful?"

I can't remember anyone ever calling me beautiful, and I felt myself blushing as I hit him and said I wasn't beautiful. We got into one of those wrestling kind of fights, and I ended up under him hugging him tight. He looked at me for a long while and stole my first kiss from me. I continued to stare at him, as he brushed my eyes and kissed my neck. His arms were strong, and his lips were soft against my skin. His lips pecked my cheeks, as his hands found their way towards my thighs . . .

That night at the party, I couldn't think of anything else. Even while I was trying to get close to this other guy, I kept thinking about Michael and what I had just done. Over the course of the next few months, I got my license, and found myself doing everything for Michael. He kept me up on the phone; we hung out almost every Saturday, and I drove him to his soccer practices. He promised me not to tell anyone, and I kept my promise. I convinced myself I loved Michael, and that somehow this was going to end up right. He sent me songs like the Beach Boys, "Wouldn't it be Nice," and the one line that always gets me is "Wouldn't it be nice if we were older, then we wouldn't have to wait so long." He was so nice to me, and I really do believe I loved him at one point.

Yes, I was the other girl.

Relationships: Isn't It Funny the Way Things Work Out?

I'm disgusted at what I was, but at the time, I was okay with it. I allowed him to walk all over me and ruin my life, because every thought that came into my head was about him. I was the other girl, and the real girl was my best friend. My best friend; the one where we got hit on together by boys who told us to hold their cups; the one who laughed with me in a hotel at Atlantic City because we could hear the couple next door having sex, who I was going to make a speech at her wedding.

I ended it with Michael, because I realized he couldn't do anything for me. I was always there for him, and he couldn't even do one single favor for me. I began to grow cold from him and distanced myself as much as I could.

Then in June, everything came crashing. Someone had found out about me and Michael, and Alyssa had threatened to tell "A," but I haven't even told Alyssa about all this, so I became a hypocrite and lied to her face about what went on. Eventually, everyone found out. It turns out I wasn't the only girl Michael was having a relationship with; he was also having sex with Ursula. All my friends turned on me, and I found myself the hermit in school for a couple of days. I felt terrible that this happened on Alyssa's birthday. I had no one to talk to; I even lost my best guy friend because of this. As immature as it sounds, he even deleted me from Myspace®. I was so alone and had no one. I found myself thinking of ways to get out of and different ways to not be around anymore.

To save you from all the drama that happened in the summer, I can give you an abridged version. All my friends eventually forgave me, even my best guy friend added me back to his Top 8. I am still a virgin, despite what this story is leading you to believe. I haven't talked to Michael for months now, unless you count that accidental time when I instant messaged him, when it was supposed to go to Alyssa. "A" has even forgiven me and is talking to me right now on how she can't believe that I just told the whole world of what happened.

Relationships can be easy or hard, depending on what you make of them

Jessica Samson

I recommend that you find the relationships in your life that will make you a positive person and let you live a good life. These many relationships build on who we are, and we can learn from all of them. We need to build healthy relationships to build healthy lives. If you just try and work at them, they can help you learn and live.

I told you; it's funny the way things work out.

# 14

# So, Did You Guys Do It Yet?

"A human should have at least 300 orgasms a year."

Sex. A million things can go though a person's mind when it is brought up; a person, a place, an emotion. Did it ever occur to you that there is a right and a wrong way of going about things? Sex can be dangerous, both physically and mentally, yet it can be amazing and one of the best ways to physically and emotionally express your true feelings for a person. Some people also look at it as fun, and if that floats your boat, then good for you. I hope to cover all of these bases in my little chapter of this book, so bear with me, and hopefully, you'll learn something.

The best advice that anyone can give is to wait. I'm not talking about waiting till marriage or anything; nowadays, many people don't get married till they're thirty; your hormones are bound to kick in way before then. Just don't rush yourself; take your time. It's never too late to do it; there's no expiration date on things like that; just pace yourself, and think things through. If you have a doubt in your mind, don't do it. If you have to think twice, don't do it. I have known many people who rush into it, without thinking things through.

Some say they want to have sex by their senior year or lose their virginity on prom night. These types of things are beyond stupidity. I don't care what religion you are or what morals you were brought up with; you lose your virginity only once! Don't just give it up because you have some friends that had sex or that "everyone else is doing it." I know twenty-year olds who are still virgins; they exist. And let's get something straight; it's not because these people aren't able, they just aren't willing to run off and throw their virginity away on some random fling. I respect that, and so should you.

However, if you are thinking about it now, first things first; protect yourself! I might sound like your mother, but I can not stress it enough. The steps in doing it are so easy, and I don't understand why anyone wouldn't. The most basic of all of these steps is to get a condom. Get a pack after school on Friday or before you go out. It doesn't matter if you're a guy or girl; your body is your responsibility, not the other person's who

Andrea Bucko

124

is sleeping with you. Remember, even if you have been with the same person for months now, you don't know what they did before you. Some people are ashamed of what they have done before you came along, and they will lie to you for as long as possible.

Another thing, you can get condoms for free these days. Go to any office of Planned Parenthood, and they'll be on the counter waiting for you. Don't be embarrassed either; honestly, knowing teens, you'll tell someone you had sex right after the deed is done and not be ashamed of it. What's the big deal if a person ringing up your purchase or the receptionist at Planned Parenthood sees you getting condoms? Now I understand if that person is your mother, but in most cases, it won't be. Keep in mind, for any of those cases, if anyone does give you a hard time, you can actually get them in trouble for it. There is no "legal age" for being able to buy condoms; some people think there are, but this is not the case.

If you're mature enough to have sex, you should be mature enough to get some condoms. Maybe I'm speaking too bluntly, but I am just being honest. This comes into play with the whole responsibility thing. If you are too nervous to get them, ask a friend or your partner to go with you. Having a buddy to hold your hand in the hallways of your elementary school made them less scary; maybe having someone next to you at the counter will offer the same effect.

I just briefly want to review what condoms actually protect you from: pregnancy, syphilis, HIV, Chlamydia, gonorrhea, genital herpes, human papillomavirus, genital warts, hepatitis and more. Do you really want to put yourself at risk of contracting any of these diseases or having a baby? Now girls, if a boy gives you an excuse for not wanting to use a condom; for example, it feels better without one, or in the time it takes to put one on he won't be able to keep it up, then he's not worth having sex with. Supposedly, not using a condom does increase sensation, but being able to pee without your crotch burning feels good, too. When it comes to your partner

*So, Did You Guys Do It Yet?*

not being able to keep it up, tell him you'll help him put it on; that should work.

Let's remember the main biological reason for having sex: to make babies. So how do we avoid this situation entirely? Well simply, don't have sex. There are two posters hanging in my health class right now. One reads, "Get into terms with your sexuality," and then has a big thing saying, "Abstain," on the bottom and gives you the definition straight out of a dictionary. The second poster has a pregnancy test on it, which reads, "This is a test you may not want to pass." One of the best ones I have ever seen was in my school's nurses' office. All it said was, "Sex can be a real scream," and it had a picture of a crying baby underneath the text. We all get the point; adults just don't want us having sex, which is understandable.

However, two thirds of all high school students graduate without their virginity, so these posters aren't really working. What schools should be teaching is how to prevent pregnancy, like the use of the pill. Now everyone should know that the pill doesn't protect against STDs and has some side effects, but it's almost 100% effective when it comes to pregnancy. Like condoms, they are available for teens; you just have to know where to go. Planned Parenthood and your local OB-GYN should be willing to help you; some of them even give them to you for free. This is something you have to do on your own, ladies. Be proactive when it comes to things like this, not reactive.

So when is the right time for your first time? Don't we all wish there were some equation where you punch in you height and weight and get the age at which to lose your virginity? That would be quite convenient; the only problem is that nothing like this exists. That kind of takes the fun out of things though. If you were to know, then there would be no point in even trying.

The biggest mistake I see made most often when it comes to having sex for the first time is people assume things. This happens most often with young couples; when a girl thinks her boyfriend wants to have sex, and if she doesn't, he'll leave her. Or a guy thinking that a girl won't think anything of him unless he forces himself on her. Communicate: if you're about to sleep with someone, you should be able to talk to them. Be on the same page as your partner; make sure you want the same things. You'll definitely feel more comfortable, and secondly, your boyfriend/girlfriend will, too. Talking brings peace of mind and more trust in a relationship. A simple conversation can make the doubt vanish from your mind, and it can go either way; you can be sure you want to do it, or you can be certain you don't. At least you will be confident and comfortable in your relationship. It makes life easier.

Now let's touch upon sex for just the blatant reason of having sex. Bad idea: I wouldn't know from experience, and I'll be honest, but I have to go with the parental units with this one. There are billions of other things you can do with another person for fun; sleeping with them doesn't have to be one of them. What will you have to resort to later in life if you start doing that now? Sex should mean a little bit more then that.

People are also very judgmental towards people who sleep around; I know I am. I will not even consider a guy worth dating if I know he sleeps around. Some people don't mind, but you're risking a lot. Many people look back at what they do and regret it. What if there's an accident? Let's say the actual biological purpose of sex occurred (a baby); what do you do? Of course, you can have an abortion, but that's not really fair for all sides of the party. Many people also have religious views against abortion, leaving only adoption or keeping the baby as options.

Another option that teens have, other then having sex but still getting rid of sexual tension is, well, masturbation. Every guy I know has "jerked himself off," some more frequently than others; maybe some are just more open about it. However, I rarely hear girls talk about it. Only one of my girlfriends has ever admitted to doing it, and she said she stopped because "she didn't like it." But why? She isn't a virgin; she likes having sex and has no problem doing it, but she can't find the will to masturbate. "Weird" is the only thing that goes through my mind, but then again, I shouldn't be saying anything. Guys are the ones that jerk off, not girls; I guess I'm sexist.

Even Dr. Oz on Oprah's television show said a human should have at least 300 orgasms a year; it is said to add up to six healthy years to your life. He did mention, however, that nothing can replace the real thing, and it works best when you have a steady sexual partner. But when one women in the audience asked, "If I don't have a sex partner, can I just do it myself?" Dr. Oz was all for it. You got to do what you have to do; what else can I say on the matter?

Another thing I remember reading in a magazine about masturbation when I was younger was about a girl who wanted to either get a vibrator or a dildo. If you didn't know, a vibrator is a little piece of plastic, that well, vibrates, and a girl can put it on her clitoris for stimulation, and a dildo is a plastic, erected penis. This girl, who was probably 16 or 17 at the time, wanted to buy one. She said she wasn't ready to have sex, but she was having sexual urges and wanted to settle them. The problem was she was scared to buy one and have her parents find it. The writer in the magazine responded and said that she could either just get one and hide it well, or talk to her parents about it and be open.

What do you think your parents would say? Mine would probably just sit there and look at me in shock. I guess some parents might be relieved; the girl did say she wasn't ready to have sex. As parents always say, "I was once your age!" They should know that teens do have sexual urges. Maybe teens do doubt their parents and their ability to reason; however, the few teens that I do know that are open with their parents about sex was because their parents opened up the door to that conversation.

Being abstinent is, of course, the best way to avoid all of these problems. If you don't have sex, you can't get pregnant, get an STD, have any emotion trauma, or any of that other baggage that shows up with the act of sex. I have

Andrea Bucko

128

respect for people who take these special oaths, especially the ones who keep their word.  The thing is that many people who take these oaths get married young.  The problem with that is, the younger you get married, the more chances of you growing apart and getting divorced.  Take Jessica Simpson for instance; maybe she's a bad example, but that's what happened to her.  She got married in her early twenties, not getting to learn about life, and then got divorced two or three years later.  So what's worse; having sex with maybe more then one person before you get married and then only marry one person when you're older, or get married young, get divorced and then sleep with more people?  The only person who can really answer that is you.

Being a virgin these days also has its many levels.  Mainly I'm talking about oral sex.  Are you still a virgin if you "went down" or "gave head" to your partner?  It's a touchy topic; some people still think you are; others say sex is sex, and if you had sex, you're not a virgin anymore.  According to Dictionary.com, to be a virgin means "a person who has never had sexual intercourse."  When you look up sexual intercourse it has two definitions; "Coitus between humans," and. "Sexual union between humans involving genital contact other than vaginal penetration by the penis."  So what this source is saying is that if you had oral sex, then you're not a virgin.  But really, who's to judge?  This debate can be stretched out beyond our imaginations.  Are you still a virgin if you hold hands, hug or kiss?  Aren't all these things somewhat sexual - a union between two people?

Another question; are you still a virgin if you fell victim to a rape attack?  You did have sexual intercourse, not by your free will, but nonetheless it happened.  You are a virgin!  You give your virginity away, not have it stolen from you.  Things that you can not control should have no effect on how other people feel about you and how you feel about yourself.  If something like a rape happens to you, be strong and take your life back; it is rightfully yours.

**So, Did You Guys Do It Yet?**

Something that can change a person's life as they get older is realizing whether they are homosexual or heterosexual; for our purposes, gay or straight.  It's fair to say it will have a major impact; many people would say it shouldn't, but the fact is, it does.  I'm not saying that one is right or wrong; they are just different.  It can be compared to whether or not you like to read or if you would rather do a math problem;  this effects what college you go to after you graduate high school and what career you might pursue after that.

Being gay or straight effects what kind of people you hang out with and might affect the relationship you have with your parents.  One of my oldest friends is a lesbian, and that's just how she is.  I met her in the sixth grade; she was kind of tomboyish, but so was I.  We got along great; I slept over her house all the time and walked home together every day.  In middle school, you can't get closer then that.  So in high school when she "came out of the closet," I wasn't even surprised because it didn't really matter.  She was still my friend, and she still is to this day.  We talk about everything, from parents to friends to significant others.  Her sexual preferences have nothing to do with our friendship.

The last thing I want to mention is talking to your parents; do it.  It might seem awkward at first, but in the long run, it can really help you out.  They were, at one point, your age, and they have gone though the things we are going through now; their advice just might help you.  If you can't speak to your parents, then try another adult.  Most teens just turn to other teens, and that's not a bad thing; however, sometimes you need more then just your best friend's advice.  There are things you will never know until you have gone through them.  Chances are, with our parents being twenty or thirty years older then us, they have gone through them.

Another reason to talk to your parents is that many parents are often willing to help out when it comes time for sex.  A few of my friends got birth control because their moms would pay for it.  It makes life easier when you don't have to

Andrea Bucko

pay for it and, on top of that, don't have to hide taking it. In addition, if you have an older boyfriend or girlfriend, check the laws in your state. It varies, but if your significant other is older then you, it can be considered rape, even if it was with your consent. This is probably more leaning toward really young kids being talked into sex, but they can still get you in trouble.

Sex is just one thing: sex. But it can branch off and split up into things that no one would even think of. You can get hurt or sick if you're not careful. It can also be one of the best experiences of your life that you will never forget. And it's not just special the first time you do; it is every time. It is the most intimate human act, and it should be. So be safe, and use caution; you will be happy you did later on.

# 15

# Are You Tryin' To Get High?

"...Is it worth watching a friend get so 'wasted' that she is puking all over herself, you, your mom's new carpet, and then having to undress her, carry her to her mother's car, and explain to her that you watched your friend get out of control and you're not sure she will wake up the next morning?"

Who doesn't like breaking the rules?  As teens, that is what we do best.  We get detention, suspension, and punishment from our parents.  Why?  We can't help but break the rules.  Drugs are no exception.  We have always been told growing up by teachers, parents, and D.A.R.E. officers that drugs are something we should have no part of.  But when we are younger, we actually listen.  We think we will never do such things.  But as we grow up, we aren't as naïve.  There are so many legal drugs, yet we choose to use them in an illegal way.  Plus, there are the drugs that start out illegal in the first place.  There can be nothing good coming from any of these drugs.  Then why do we take them?

To get high is to experience something like no other.  We can escape reality, even if it's just for a second.  But when we snap out of it, we are left with all our old problems and more.  How can this be healthy?  All these people in rehab and hospitals, I'm sure they all wanted to escape what was going on in their life.  But look now.  They have so much more to worry about.  Now they can't even function without drugs.  How healthy is that?

Cocaine, Heroine, Marijuana, Methamphetamine, Acid, Mushrooms, Ecstasy, Alcohol.....bake it, smoke it, shoot it, sniff it, eat it, snort it, lick it, melt it, drink it, swallow it.  There is so much to do with so many illegal substances.  So why do we bring common items into the mix?  With so many choices of illegal drugs, why use household or drug store legal things?  Oh yea, less expensive, right, keep the world on its toes.  I walked into Walgreens to get cold medicine with a friend, and I'm looked at like a drug addict.  They are thinking; what are you going to do with that?  Smoke it, shoot it, eat it, snort it, swallow it?  No man, I'm just trying to get over this cold.  Or even purchasing a can of Lysol for my car.  The cashier is thinking, are your going to put that in a bag and sniff that?  You're going to get high? Sick kids, why should I sell this to you?  I just want to tell them to chill out; my car smells, I need it.  But I guess in the society we live in, this is a major concern.  A simple medicine like Robitussin® can't even be purchased

Angela Nascondiglio

by anyone under 18. People are drinking it by the bottle like it's water.

So what happens when you take any of these drugs? It feels pretty good. It gives you something to do with your friends on the weekend. You get a few laughs, a few memories, or maybe even some romance. But is it worth it? Is it worth watching your best friend make out with your boyfriend right in front of your face? Is it worth getting into that fight that if you were sober, you knew you would have never started? Is it worth looking at that picture of you, lying on the floor, passed out, with words and pictures drawn all over your body. Is it worth watching a friend get so "wasted" that she is puking all over herself, you, your mom's new carpet, and then having to undress her, carry her to her mother's car, and explain to her that you watched your friend get out of control, and you're not sure she will wake up the next morning. It's not worth it. I have been through all of those things. Let me say, that the 20 minutes to a 3 hour good feeling we get, is not worth a lifelong consequence.

We've all made a lot of terrible decisions in our time. Some of our livers probably look like shriveled up cucumbers, and our lungs are probably black as night. We kill so many brain cells and erase most of our common sense. We've stopped caring about many things that call for attention. We wait for the weekends to have fun with our friends. That's all we talk about all week is how we are going to get wasted on the weekend. It's a sick, unhealthy obsession. Why do we think it's so fun? What is so wrong with reality that we have to escape it? The sad thing is that all these drugs are so easy for us to obtain. We go to a local liquor store to purchase alcohol. Each of us has about four people in our phone books to call for drugs like marijuana, cocaine, and ecstasy. We have the choice every weekend. It's like a restaurant. What would you like this evening? All of our money from our jobs, parents, grandparents, it's all going towards damaging our health. And when, and if, we go a weekend without doing any type of drug, the next weekend gets double the amount. We are giving this money to the people who don't even deserve it. Should we be giving our money to the dealers who are getting arrested, spreading addiction, and getting our hard-earned money while doing no work at all? And, half of these people that are dealing aren't even taking the drug themselves. They've seen all the addicted people and don't want to spend their money on the drugs. They are using our screw ups to better themselves. They view us as the stupid ones. Think about that next time you make a call.

Long-term effects of drugs we face are risks of heart attacks, strokes, brain damage, seizures, and so much more. The immediate effects of drugs are just as bad as the long-term ones. Who knows what will happen to us as we use these substances? I can see it now. The headline reading "Teen Dies from Alcohol Poisoning," or something to that effect. We see it every day. I know people who have watched their friends die right in front of them and could do nothing about it. I've even been close myself. Countless times I've seen people have a little too much "fun," and pass out. I've said to many friends the next day, "I didn't know if you were going to get up this morning." I'm sure they are thinking; well, thank you for stopping me. But, it's our choice, and who are we going to count on? We have to be responsible to save our friends and family from the possible grief and agony.

Drugs can keep you from participating in your regular events. I play three varsity sports, and although nothing has stopped me from succeeding, I have seen many people fall due to drugs. Depending on what you take, they can make you tired, weak, not in shape, or make you lose your concentration. When you are addicted to a drug, you think of nothing else. Plus, if you do play sports competitively, you might become interested in steroids, which are illegal to take during these activities. There have been so many cases of great athletes that were found to have taken steroids. After that, their reputations were ruined, and no one looked p to them anymore. Sure, the pressure gets to us and we want to succeed, but taking steroids will just cause failure.

Angela Nascondiglio

Certain drugs cause different symptoms. When you mix these drugs, you are mixing their effects. If you mix an energy drink with vodka, you heart rate increases with the caffeine from the drink and slows down because of the alcohol. This just sounds bad. People are dying from this mixture. We are not being careful enough about what we are choosing to do. Of course, we shouldn't be doing any drugs at all. But doing more than one at a time? I've seen people pop seven ecstasy pills at one time. Yes, it's the same drug, but seven of them? Do you know what that does to your body? I have friends that have taken the whole box of triple C's, fifteen pills, and then drank a whole 40 oz. of beer. Carried away? Yes, to the extreme. Imagine what possesses people to do these things and what kind of effects it has?

There are unhealthy affects of drugs that aren't necessarily lethal or dangerous but just unhealthy. One of the most common drugs among teens is marijuana. Marijuana gives you what is called the munchies, which means you get very hungry. I've seen people eat enough food for twelve in ten minutes all by themselves. If you smoke regularly, that's pounds and pounds of food every day. This will cause you to gain so much weight. Plus, I'm sure it's not carrots or apples you are going to grab when you're munching. It's the unhealthy food we want. If you look at it from the other side, cocaine makes people lose their appetites. This can cause serious eating disorders and serious weight loss.

I bet if you asked every person you saw on the street if they have ever used drugs, probably one out of every thirty would say no. I think that's crazy. Look at your little brother, sister, cousin, niece, nephew, son, daughter, or friend. At one point in their life, they are going to try some sort of drug. Doesn't that make you sad? I get a chill every time I think of it. The people we care about are going to get physically hurt, and what are we going to do about it? Half of our parents don't even have a clue what we are doing to ourselves. If someone went up to their mother, looked her straight in the eye, and told her everything they have done, I think she would cry. If someone were to say, "Mom, I'm sorry I get drunk every weekend. I'm sorry I smoke pot. I'm sorry I've tried ecstasy. I'm sorry I snorted cocaine. I'm sorry I overdosed on caffeine pills. I'm sorry I smoke cigarettes. I'm sorry I can't promise you I'll never do it again. I'm sorry I'm hurting this life you have given me." I think she would look her child in the eyes and cry. My mother would. She gave me life. Our parents gave us this gift. And we are hurting ourselves. The people that love us watch us crumble. But friends aren't people that just sit back and watch. True friends don't let their friends die. If we are so-called "friends," how come we don't tell each other not to do wrong, unhealthy things? I fall victim to this. Sometime, I don't tell friends what it is that's wrong, I join them in the act. But I am not being loyal. We cannot continue to watch people crumble. I have had friends approach me, telling me the choices I am making are wrong. At first, of course, I didn't want to listen to them. But I am thankful now that they saved me. We must be the ones to stop a tragedy before it happens.

Many have had the worst consequence of all. Some people have died. Then why haven't we learned? It's so expensive to have this addiction, this love for a high. Everyone who does at least one drug frequently is addicted. I am addicted, my parents are addicted, my brothers are addicted, my friends are addicted, and you, although you may have no idea, are probably addicted. It ruins a lot. I've watched so much happen. We even see our supposed role models on TV and movies that are addicted to these drugs we are taught not to take. How are we, as teenagers, going to listen to people tell us not to do drugs if the people we look up to are doing them?

So many people have fallen. We all need help to just get back up. We all reach for help in one way or another. We all need help. No one takes this seriously enough, including me especially. There are many rehab programs for teens like us, but no one wants to admit that they have a problem. It is the most innocent looking, good kids that may be the ones in need of help. So how can we tell? We can't. The person must

Angela Nascondiglio

be willing to get help before it is given. If someone comes to you for help, then we can start towards getting them treatment.

If this is such a common problem, what can we do to fix it? Well, for one, we can start respecting ourselves and our bodies. Whether you are a Christian, Catholic, Buddhist, Atheist, or whatever, you still need to have morals and stick to them. If your parents taught you right and wrong as a child, why wouldn't we listen? Even if you once didn't know it was wrong, now you do. It is true that the heart desires wrong over right, but we can overcome this. A wise man once said, "To admit you are wrong is simply being wiser today than you were yesterday." You have to make some mistakes to learn from them. So if we are choosing to harm our bodies with drugs or are watching someone else harm himself, then why aren't we learning from it? We see celebrities and TV show characters struggle with and get hurt from drugs and alcohol. So why don't we take this example and learn from it?

The truth is, as kids we don't want to admit we are wrong. My favorite thing to say to people is, "I do what I want when I want. I'm grown." But really, this is the farthest from the truth. We are still so young and inexperienced. There is so much for us to learn as young adults. We have to stop being so hard headed and get over the fact that we aren't always right. We need to listen to elder's advice.

Some people have serious problems with addiction. Others aren't in too deep. If you are seriously addicted or harmed, you need professional help. My best friend dated a boy that went to counseling every week for his marijuana abuse problems. He thought it was bogus and that he didn't need help. Having this attitude made him not get better and continue on his negative path. So having a positive attitude and being willing to learn is very important for teens. If we don't want help, we can't receive it.

To not start these problems in the first place, we have to occupy our time. Teens may start doing drugs because there is nothing better to do. If you develop a hobby or get involved in extracurricular activities, you may have less chance in getting involved in drugs or alcohol. Playing sports or getting involved in a club will occupy your time and give you less time to worry about other things. Also, we need to have or create more things in our community to do on nights and weekends. Holding dances or having a movie theater around town will give teens something to do on their nights off, instead of putting harmful substances in their bodies.

Surrounding ourselves with positive influences is also a very important thing. If our friends or family members are doing these harmful things, we soon will, too. We can't deny this. We may think that if they do something; we still have the ability to resist. This is true, but very hard to do. A friend of mine's mother smoked cigarettes. In eighth grade, she stole her mom's cigarettes and decided to try smoking. She picked up the habit. Then, she brought it to our group of friends. Now, most of my friends smoke. It's amazing what one person can bring to a group. Whether it is positive or negative, peer pressure is highly effective. If someone you are surrounded by constantly is doing something, you too will start to develop this. Think about it this way. Has there ever been a certain trademark word or phrase you've used in the past? Have you ever been talking to a friend or overhearing a conversation and heard this word or phrase out of their mouth? It is because they are so used to being around you, they have this word or phrase in their vocabulary. They are used to hearing this, so it develops in them. It becomes okay to use and say. This is the same with harmful things, such as drugs and alcohol.

We, as teens, should also have people in our life to help us make good decisions. I have one friend who I consider my best. Every time I mess up, she's the first one to tell me. She is not afraid to do so. She also shows me how good making the right choices are by her actions. Every time I am faced with a problem, I think of what she would do, and I turn to her for advice. This is what we need. As teens, there are so many people out there waiting for us to fall. There needs to be those good people in your life to pick you back up and set you on the

Angela Nascondiglio

right path.  This can be a friend, family member, or a belief in a higher power.

I play three varsity sports, get good grades, take challenging courses, and am a great friend, daughter, and sister.  I consider myself a good role model.  So when I mess up, I feel like I let other down who look up to me.  We have to see that there are others who look up to us.  There are people who need us for advice and to be used as an example.  We must think of others as well as ourselves.  How would your little brother or sister feel if they saw their big sibling messing with drugs?  Would they want to do it, too?  Would they be disappointed?  Would they learn to hate you?  Would they want to be like you?  We need to consider this.  No one wants to be looked at as a loser.

We also must think about whom we view as role models.  Like I said before, people look up to me because I play sports and get good grades.  But yet, I make really bad choices.  You may look up to a singer or actor and think, "Wow, they are really cool.  Look at their clothes and hair.  Look at how much money they are making.  I wish I looked and acted just like them."  Yet, these people may snort one hundred dollars' worth of cocaine every night, take pills to calm their anxieties, and drink heavily at parties.  Then you may look at them and think, "See they do all of this, yet they are still successful.  It's okay that I am doing this, too."  Or, you may think, "Maybe this is how I can get noticed and receive attention."  No matter how successful, beautiful, or popular someone is, this does not make them a good role model.  As teens, we can be misled so easily.  We need to be more careful of whom we look up to.

Most importantly, we have to remember the consequences of our actions.  The only way to prevent drug use and be high on life is thinking about what can happen.  Take a shot of that vodka, then how are you going to get home?  Are you going to drive?  Yes, get behind that wheel, hit another car, kill them, kill yourself, and hurt all those living in grief.  Steal your mother's money to get that ecstasy pill.  You buy it, swallow it, feel the high.  But your mom can't buy your lunch for the next day.  She doesn't know where she misplaced the money.  She gets upset.  She takes it out on herself.  She feels like a bad mother.  These things can happen, but maybe they don't.  But, are you willing to take that risk?  Are you willing to deal with the consequences?  If we think about how what we do will affect people, maybe we won't do bad things.  Maybe that's all we need to do before every choice we make.  Just sit and think; can I deal with what might happen?  I bet the amount of drug use and harmful choices would decrease.  But, teens move too fast.  We don't take the time to think.  We don't care to know what will happen.  We don't want to face reality.  And, my friends, that is why we want to escape this reality in the first place.  So we use drugs.  Make sense?  I think not...

Angela Nascondiglio

# 16

# Are You Confident?

"What every young woman and man should know is that you should LOVE THE SKIN YOUR IN. It does not matter what size you are. In order to be confident about yourself, you first have to love yourself."

When you look at your reflection in the mirror, what do you see? Do you see a confident person, or do you see a scared timid person? These days, teenagers are pressured to look a certain way or eat a certain way to fit into society. Everyday we hear about new fads that take over the way we live. It is either we should look like this or we should look like that. It's as if we have to live by a certain standard in order to fit in with everybody else. Usually we hear, "Oh, he/she is too skinny, or she is too fat." For some people, there is no in-between. Either you are at one end of the spectrum or on the other end. We all have these preconceived notions about what looks good and what doesn't. That is what usually kills us when it comes to our appearance.

When it comes to diet and health, the main factor teenagers should concentrate on is confidence. It is the key that opens doors for us. There is even more pressure as a teenager to live in this world. We get so worked up about what is happening on the outside that we forget to think about what's going on in the inside. There are so many things that distract us, and in the end, we realize that we have ignored all of the important factors. One of these factors would be our confidence levels. We can talk about anything in this world except our confidence, especially when in comes to our diet and health.

Most teenagers are not satisfied with the way they look, the way they eat, or their health. Some of them even go so far that they become a threat to themselves. Those who cannot speak up about what they feel, usually bottle their feelings all inside and pretend that everything is alright. Their confidence levels are so low, and they think that there is nothing that they can do about it. Instead of taking charge of their health and appearance, they mope around, feeling sorry for themselves and wish that they could be someone else. At some point in our lives, we have all felt that way, but we did not want anyone to know. I am writing to reassure you that you are not alone, and there is nothing wrong with you.

Juliana Boateng

Because we think so negatively, we feel that there is nothing that can be done about the situation. Well we thought wrong. Beginning with yourself and with help from others, you can change that preconceived thought. You can become that person you want to be, with confidence. You can hold up your head high wherever you go, because you have become that confident person, and people will begin look at you with respect.

Confidence can work wonders for an individual, especially teenagers. Most of you have come to a period in your life where you are so conscious about your weight and how you look. Do not stress out because everybody is different. You may bring yourself down because you do not look the way you would like to. That should not be the case. There are many ways to build up your confidence, starting with the way you carry yourself in and out of school. We may look at ourselves differently than our friends do. When they give compliments like, "You look cute today," or "I like your outfit," it gets us thinking about what they really mean by that comment. You might think, "Oh, then what about the rest of the days when I am not dressed up? Are they trying to say that I don't look cute on other days?" All these negative thoughts run through our heads. A confident person would just take the compliment and leave it as it is.

You're probably wondering what all of this has to do with diet and health. If you think about it, it is very much related to our diet and health. Not only does it have to do with physical health, but mental health as well. In order to achieve confidence about ourselves physically, we have to achieve mental confidence. It is not always about the physical aspect.

You may think, "How can I boost my confidence levels about the way I look or the way I eat"? First, we have to discuss what we eat because that plays a significant role in confidence. We are teenagers, so we usually eat all the wrong foods. We go out to eat at McDonald's®, Burger King®, White Castle®, or Taco Bell®. Most of us eat at these fast food places morning, noon, and night. It is completely unhealthy,

Are You Confident?

but some of us cannot control ourselves. When the pounds starts packing, that's when it becomes a problem for those who eat those types of food. In order to feel confident about yourself, you have to watch what you eat. I am not saying that you should go out and starve yourselves. We'll discuss that later. I am saying that the foods we eat have an effect on teenagers.

When was the last time you sat down to a healthy meal that you created yourself? Think about it. In most cafeterias, there are always a variety of foods that are unhealthy, always calling out your name to buy them. Instead of giving in into those temptations, it would be best to walk away from them. Walking away from that unhealthy product could help your confidence because then you know that if you were to face that situation again, you could just walk away. It won't be as hard to give into that temptation as it was before.

Eating the right foods has a great impact on your confidence level. When you eat right, you feel good about yourself. You don't have to worry about counting up the calories in everything that you eat. Not only do you feel great, but your body also is also delighted. It gets the nutrition that it needs, and in return, it provides energy. Physically, when you start to eat right, you may see changes in your body. You may even look slimmer than you usually do. By eating the right foods, you are also ensuring your health for the future. Once these good eating habits become permanent, you won't have a problem with your health. When you are older, you will also have a low chance of having any life-threatening illnesses.

Eating the right foods is half the factor for becoming confident in your appearance. You will also have to exercise to get your body the way you would want it to be. I'm not saying go and exercise eight hours daily. I'm talking about little things. Instead of driving everywhere, you could try walking from place-to-place. Even walking to school if your home is not that far can count as exercise for the day. Instead of talking the elevator in a building, you could climb up the stairs. There are so many ways to fit exercise into our day, so it will not

Juliana Boateng

disrupt our daily plans. Not only will you notice a difference in your health, but also in your confidence level. People will also notice the changes in your attitude and in the way you present yourself.

Physical appearance these days is everything. When you turn on the TV, there are always commercials for new diet plans or diet pills. You see the smaller size people in these commercials and think, "Wow, he or she looks really good." Society, especially TV, brings up the standards on how to look. It gets teenagers wondering why they do not look like that. Teenagers are most likely to go and take the initiative to go change their body types in order to fit in to what is "right." We all want to look like the TV image, but we can't.

"Everybody in Hollywood is doing it, so it is okay for me to do it also;" "Why can't I look like that?" "Why was I born this way?" "Why do I have to have this or that?" These are all questions that go through your minds when it comes to your physical appearance. You think that everybody looks this way, so you have to look that way too or else you won't fit into the crowd. You watch TV and see shows like America's Next Top Model or the Janice Dickenson agency, and you become depressed. Your confidence drops because you think that you don't look like those models, so no one will accept you. It is hard to find ways to overcome what you're feeling, so you start to do things for sympathy. I know when I am feeling bad or down, I take a container of ice cream and sit in front of the TV until the container is done. Others may lock themselves in a room and will not come out. Many turn to drastic measure to get to the image that they want. Teenagers, the majority of them females, turn to starving themselves or throwing up what they eat. They may think that nobody likes them because of the way they look. In the end, they end up endangering their health and put their lives on the line just so society will accept them.

Many teenage females are very insecure about themselves, especially their weight. In America, females are supposed to be slender and small. If you look around America today, you will not see slender girls but those who are on the plus size. A survey that was done on the "Tyra Banks Show," yielded results that the average American woman was a size twelve. So what does that tell you? Not everybody in this world is skinny. Some would consider that big, but in reality, it is not. I wear a size twelve in petite, but when I tell people that, they don't believe me. They usually think that I am size eight or a ten. I usually laugh in their face when they say that, but it makes me feel good to know that I look smaller than what I actually am.

Young women need to realize that it is not about what society thinks is right, but it is about what they think is right. It all deals with confidence and how you present yourself to others. In a bathing suit, bigger girls will feel insecure about their weight in the suit, but it should not matter; as long as they feel comfortable, and they think they look good, it should not matter what other people say. A new kind of woman is emerging to the surface, and it is not a fat women. She is plus sized and thick. When it comes to women, there is no such thing as being fat. It is either you're skinny, average, thick, and/or plus size. Calling a woman fat is being very disrespectful, and it can lower her confidence and the way she thinks about herself.

You should not be calling people names because of their weight. They won't show you any emotion; when they are in private is when all the emotion will come out. People may come across as nothing bothers them. Most of the time, it is a cover-up on how they really feel. For example, a plus sized teenager will make jokes about herself, so people can laugh with her and not at her. When she goes home, that is when she will unwind and show her true feelings about herself. She lacks confidence because she is afraid that if she is herself, then nobody will like her. We don't think that these situations occur, but they do daily.

Some girls even try to cover themselves up by layering clothing item-by-item. They do not want anybody to know how they really look. Putting more clothes on would not be the

Juliana Boateng

solution. Young ladies need to learn how to embrace their bodies. Some may think that their body is their curse, but in reality, it is not. Your body is a work of art that should be appreciated and taken care of. As appreciation for the body rises, so does confidence. You should not be afraid to show yourself a little. My friend used to tell me, "Use what your mother gave you," and that is what I have been doing ever since. Before I reached where I am at this point in time, I was not even close to appreciating my body. I used to run track and cross country, so I had an athlete's figure. The year I decided that I was not going to play any sports; I ended up gaining weight. At first, I tried to cover it up because I did not like the way I looked. As time went on, I learned to love my body because it is a huge part in confidence. Also when I took AP Psychology, we learned that everybody has a set point. It is the weight range in which your body is programmed to weigh and will fight to maintain that weight. Ever since I reached my set point, I've only gained a pound, and that was a couple years ago. Now that I have started eating healthy again, I feel a difference in my body physically and mentally.  When I go out now, I hold my head up and carry myself well because I know that I feel good, and nobody can take that away. What gets me the most is when people find out what I actually weigh, they don't believe me. They think that I am much smaller then what I say.

It is okay to weigh more than what you look like, especially if you eat right and exercise daily. Muscle weighs more than fat. So if you're trying to lose weight, but you end up gaining weight and you are smaller, it is just the muscle weight taking place of the fat. Trust me, I don't care about the weight that much because I know that I look good, so why should I have to complain? I am very confident because I have learned to work with what I have instead of hiding it from everyone else.

What every young woman should know is that you should LOVE THE SKIN YOU'RE IN. It does not matter what size you are. In order to be confident about yourself, you first have to love yourself. Sometimes it may not come easy but it can be worked on. Everyday you females wake up, go to the mirror and say, "I am fearfully and wonderfully made." This phrase is a great confidence booster. When you stand in the mirror and say positive things about yourself, it is reassuring yourself that you really are all the things you are saying. As days pass by, you will probably see a difference in the way that you think and act. You won't be afraid to go out into the world and worry about what others think about you because you are the only person that knows you. Your eyes will open to new objects in life that you never knew existed. Burdens will be lifted off your shoulders. Just think how nice it would be to wake up in the morning and not have to worry about what problems that may occur in the day.

Other females will do just about anything to try and fit in, even if it means tampering with their health. Males also go through this because they to want be accepted into the society. Those who are not very confident about themselves tend to be easily swayed by anything they hear or told to do. All they know is that if they do what they are told, then they will be accepted. These situations often happen in school. The kids who are well-known will single out a person. Most of the time, it is just for fun, and on other occasions, they want somebody to do their dirty work for them. Once the student is singled out, and then they pretend to become friends with that person until the student feels that the other party can be trusted. As time goes on, the well-known student will keep on saying, "You know that I am your friend," or something along those lines to encourage him or her. The student will continue to believe that, and when he or she is asked to do something small, they do it. Time passes on, and the tasks become more difficult and challenging. It will reach that point when the well known kid will offer the non-confident student drugs, and he or she, thinking that this is their friend, will take them.

Sooner or later, that student who did not have confidence is now on drugs and their health is deteriorating Their condition can become worse, or if they chose to, they

Juliana Boateng

can try to stop the drugs and put their lives back on track. But this is just an example of what lack of confidence can persuade you to do. If we do not exhibit some kind of confidence as we go through our daily lives, we can be taken advantage of by others, and it can lead to bad health conditions.

Teenagers should not be swayed by the nonsense of someone who really does not care about you. A real friend would not offer you drugs or anything that would be dangerous to your health. That is why teenagers have to build up their confidence, especially when it comes to image. If another person sees that you're a weakling, they will say anything to try and take advantage of you. It mostly happens with females. Nobody, including yourself, tells you how great you look or that you are beautiful. You can get sidetracked by a boy who tells you all the sweet things that you have not heard before. You start to think that he really likes you, and he is serious about you, but that is not always the case. This can go on for weeks or even months. Sooner or later, he'll ask you for something that you're not sure you want to give up. He will say that he loves you, or he cares about you, and you might fall right into his trap. When it's over and done with, he doesn't want to speak to you or even look at you. It is then that you will realize that he was just using you and he got what he wanted. Now what do you do? You fell into his trap because you did not have confidence, and he took advantage of the situation. This all leads up to stress, depression, or low self esteem.

Stress about confidence can be terrible to your health. Because we worry all the time about what we think others think about us. It drains you, and you feel tired all the time because of it. Stress can lower confidence. Usually it becomes nerve racking to know that others are talking about you behind your back. We can get so worked about sometimes that it affects the way we eat. Our meals don't become meals anymore but little snacks. It is as if the world is upon your shoulders weighing you down. The burdens of stress become very heavy that you sometimes lose confidence in your ability to perform the task ahead of you. Instead of sleeping, you stay up all night and think about all the little things that you have to do. One thing that you must know is that stress is a killer. It can lead up to different types of depression.

One type would be SAD or Seasonal Affective Disorder. This is when you become depressed, especially in the winter months because the days are much shorter. It is also caused by imbalance in the brain with the level of serotonin that we receive. Symptoms include feeling tired all the time, not wanting to socialize with others, a loss of appetite and more. There are ways to treat SAD, and one of them would be light therapy. Light therapy would be sitting by a bright source of light to imitate the brightness the sun gives of during the longer days of the year. Other would include nutrition and awareness. It is always good to keep up with the nutrition because that is the important part. Eating the right foods can make a difference in the way we feel. Nutrition is the stepping stone in order to get your life back. Once you begin to eat the right foods, your confidence level will start to rise because you can trust yourself to look after what you eat.

Nutrition is always they key to confidence which is the key to a healthier life. We cannot ignore the fact that it determines the way we live. If our nutrition is bad, then our health will be bad and our confidence will drop. If our nutrition is good, then our health will be good, and we will see our confidence rise. It all depends on whether or not we have the will to take control of our lives in order to boost our confidence.

Now guys, don't think that I forgot about you. It is also important for guys to be confident in their health also. There is also pressure on your part to live to what society desires and what women desire. Middle school and high school is usually when awareness about their appearance and their health kicks in. The mindset of a male is completely opposite the mindset of a female. Guys tend to want to get bigger in size, while ladies tend to what to lose weight. Either way, they both require the element of confidence.

Juliana Boateng

Usually guys want to hit the gym and build up muscle to show off. There is a healthy way for this to be done, and there are the dangerous ways. Society has put pressure on guys to be physically fit because they are the "stronger sex".

The guys want to look good for the girls and for their friends. Most likely, if a guy is amongst his friends, he would want to show of for them to see that he is built. Also when girls walk by during a hot summer day, guys want to be confident on how they look, so that they can attract the girls' attention.

Most teenage boys only care about sports. There are usually the football, basketball, soccer, and baseball teams that are paid the most attention to. Guys aspire to look like their favorite player or play like their favorite player. This can sometimes lead to extreme measures to achieve that look. Some guys will do it the right way and will work out daily and eat right. Others will probably use steroids to enhance their performance. Sometimes there may be added pressure to use steroids. The whole team can be counting on you to lead them, but you know that you are not physically capable to do so. To build up stamina and enhance performance, you take the steroids, and you notice a difference in yourself. You continue to use the drugs, but you do not realize the harm that it is causing.

A confident young man would have realized that this is not the right way to go about the situation. He would have thought about the idea in the first place.

This decision would save the young man's health and whatever future that would be ahead of him. Now, young men supposedly body build so that they can show off all the muscles on their bodies. Too much of it can actually stunt your growth. That is not healthy for young men. All you have to remember is to keep a well-balanced nutrition and work out correctly. The confidence package will increase in return.

# Afterword

"Spill the ink and spill your guts again..."
-Hidden in Plain View – Garden Statement.

It all started in September, and my class and I got to choose between two book reports or writing one of our own; I'm fairly certain you can figure out which one we chose. It has been an interesting road since that fateful day: fundraising, organizing, and planning.

I had the privilege of being named General Manager. It was a lot of work but completely worth it. I was a part of every decision that was made to create this book, and I cannot wait to see it in all its glory. The stories are real; they are ours, from our hearts and for you to share.

Even though the class never agreed on anything unanimously, I can say with confidence that we are proud to have our names on the cover and our stories imprinted on its pages. This is a book anyone can benefit from and is written by people who truly wanted to share their stories with you. We want you to have it a little easier then we did. Even if we affect you in the slightest way, that would make it worth our while.

# About the Authors

Arielle Cannon
    Arielle Cannon is currently a senior at Union High School. While her first passion is history, she also enjoys writing and inspiring her peers in a positive way. In the future, she plans to obtain a degree in child psychology, where she will use it to build her own children's enrichment clinic, especially for the less fortunate. Arielle enjoys baking, any sport that has to do with water, and church. One word of advice that she would like to share with those who read this book is to never let someone talk you out of dreams, no matter how far-fetched they may seem.

Steven Le
    Steven Le is a senior of Union High School, graduating in June 2008. He is pursuing a career in molecular biology, biotechnology, or bioengineering. Like his chapter on myths and facts, he wishes to be part of the solution. By his career interests, he aspires to cure cancer, to eradicate today's deadliest diseases, and to give all humans better lives through advanced biotechnology. Other than his aspirations, his hobbies include listening to music, spending time with friends, and creating animated movies under the Machinima genre; you may view them at http://www.youtube.com/slproductions

Raahi Upadhyay
    Hey everyone!  My name is Raahi Upadhyay and I am a senior at Union High School!  My high school experience has been extremely interesting and I probably will never forget it.  I have grown a lot during these years and I am proud of the person I am now.  Like all of you, I have gone through the "growing pains" of life and will continue to go through them.  My chapter will make it much easier for you to handle these growing pains.  Ok so enough of my chapter, let's talk about me!  I am Indian and am proud of it.  I do not know much about my religion and culture but I try to take every opportunity

I have to learn about it. I would rather have two great friends then a whole bunch of friends. I would pick love over anything. I am going to major in biochemistry in college and hope to one day become a cardiologist. Everyone has their own unique personality but it is important to keep this as your own. Never lose your individuality and this is exactly what my chapter is trying to make all of you understand. Basically, always be a first-rate version of yourself instead of a second rate version of some body else.

## Carnita Tyler

Hello everyone my name is Carnita Tyler. I am from Newark, NJ and currently a senior at Union High School. Writing this book has given me a great opportunity to express my feelings and thoughts on the Foster Care Health System. I hold no one responsible for the events that have occurred in my life while in foster care. I hope that after reading this you will begin to live life to its fullest and take nothing for granted. LOVE. LIFE. PEACE.

## Celeste Schimmenti

I'm Celeste Schimmenti, author of the chapter on mental health. I have, well, a busy life, so obviously I have experience struggling with my own sanity, yet I still manage to be the most easy going person you can meet. Life is exactly what you want it to be, so make the most of it and don't miss out. Why dwell on the negative when you can go out and have some fun? Love with all your heart, live with all your energy, and don't worry, everything eventually brightens up!

## Adrienne S. Bednarz

Adrienne Stephanie Bednarz is a student from the Graduating Class of 2008 at Union High School. She hopes to pursue International Relations and Translation in order to be able to work for the European Union as well as help people. She has traveled to many places, touched upon all continents except for Australia, extensively traveling throughout Asia,

Southeast Asia and Europe. Throughout her travels she has talked to people from different cultures and reached an understanding with them, even though she doesn't speak their language. As a result of this traveling, she has been inspired to do something that will help change people's lives across the world as well as make other people aware of other cultures and cultural differences. Her favorite hobbies are writing, reading, photography, horseback riding, swimming, and scuba diving. It was a pleasure to write the chapter, from which she hopes that you have learned a lot and has impacted your life in some way, giving you hope for survival through the worse parts. She says, "Remember, a negative attitude is not going to help you. You have to be strong, tough, and with a smile on your face, taking whatever life throws your way with a positive attitude, because in the end you will make it through—but life isn't fair. There is a saying that goes "A Journey of a Thousand Miles begins with a Single Step," and no one ever said that this journey will be easy, but you have to make that step and go on." If you wish to contact her, you can find her on Facebook®.

## Vincent Michael Imbornone

## Oluwatosin Oluyadi

My name is Oluwatosin Fareedat Oluyadi. I was born on May 19, 1990, in my native country, Nigeria. This is where I spent most of my childhood. My family moved to Saudi Arabia. Here I attended a British International School. I moved to New Jersey, when I was thirteen. I have one younger brother, called Bayaan. I am currently a senior in Union High School. My goals and aspirations are to become a pediatrician and establish my own charity health organization for underprivileged children. One of my favorite hobbies is to look after children, and hopefully I will have some of my own some day.

## Kristen Murdoch

Kristen Murdoch, author of Exercise: What's The Point?, is true to her chapter. She is an avid equestrian and long distance runner. Kristen hopes to study communications and equine science at college next year. Kristen's always outgoing, feel free to facebook her! Enjoy the book!"

## Wislande Guillaume

Look at the world with fresh eyes every day and be happy to be alive. Look outside, breath in the fresh air, and just live. Run around the streets or jump up and down. Do whatever your heart desires just don't put limitations on yourself. The worst thing that I know that I have done to myself was put limitations on myself for what I could and couldn't do. I assumed that since I was bad at something then there was no point in trying because it would not make a difference. I learned the hard way that having that kind of attitude was a big mistake, from that point on I realized that the possibilities were endless. There were so many things that I could do and become in this world; therefore, there was no point in limiting what my future could be because failure is a part of life. If nobody failed then how could success be achieved. In the end, all I can do is, not limits myself with definitions, categories, labels, or agendas. I create freely, I live unrestrained, and I explore the possibilities.

## Reshma Niyamathullah

Hey guys! I'm Reshma Niyamathullah and currently a senior at Union High School reppin' the class of 2008! I'm one of the most outgoing people you can ever meet... just living my life to the fullest each and everyday. My four years at UHS have definitely helped me develop as a unique individual, and I owe all my thanks to my family, friends, and teachers. Living your life without giving back to the community is pointless which is why I wish to pursue a career in the medical field in the future. I want to make a difference in the lives of others in order for me to be the change that I am passionately yearning to see in the world. Writing my chapter on being overweight and unhappy is one of the greatest accomplishments of my life because I am sure that it will change the lives of teenagers for the better. We're only young once... so remember, there is nothing more important in life than being your own individual, taking chances, and making mistakes. Live the life that you love and love the life that you live!

## Kadeisha Kilgore
Dear Readers,
     My name is Kadeisha. I am a determined, hard-working, inquisitive, and intellectually curious African-American young lady. I love to dance, read, and play soccer. In the near future I want to be a pediatrician, and I want to specialize in oncology (the branch of medicine that studies cancer) because two people that are very close two me died from cancer, and I know others who have this disease. My second dream career is modeling. I really want to go on America's Next Top Model, so maybe you may see me someday, and vote for me for Cover Girl of the Week (lol). I chose to write this chapter because eating disorders afflict so many people, especially teenagers, and models too. Why lose your life because you don't eat properly? It doesn't make sense, you have to take care of the body that God gave you. I wanted to share what I know about eating disorders, while motivating people to do what is most important, and that is to love yourself for who you are on the inside.
Happy Reading!
     Kadeisha

## Jessica Samson
     Jessica Ann Samson is a senior at Union High School and is continuing her education in New York City to major in Communications. Although her chapter on relationships may present her to society as a total nutcase, she will be okay. She has decided to stop trying to find the meaning of life because every time she does, they change it. She plans on living her

dreams and finishing her "Things to do Before I Die" list. And no, it's not Jessica Simpson, it's Jessica Samson.

Angela Nascondiglio
Yes, I am the Angela Nascondiglio (yes, that's 12 letters). I guess my story isn't too interesting. I am fortunate to have two loving parents, two crazy brothers, a good family, great friends, and a happy life. I have played three varsity sports for my high school since I was a freshman. I am a very outgoing, funny girl who just wants everything to be okay all the time. I just like to have fun. I get good grades, get all my work done, and am nineteenth in a class of six hundred and seventy five. I try my hardest to get everyone's approval, although I shouldn't. I enjoy life and all things that are given to me. I guess you can say I have been pretty spoiled so far. My friends call me the tin man because I'm not good with emotions, but I do have a big heart. I am not very accepting of new things, but I try. I am just a teenager like all the rest of you trying to find my way. I wish you all the best of luck trying to find yours. 08 till I die!

Andrea Bucko
My name is Andrea Bucko, and yes, the last name is real. I am a suburban girl with big plans and even bigger dreams. I live for the moment and can't wait till college (Stevens c/o 2012!!). I wish you all the best, and if you feel, for some reason, the urge to talk, Facebook me, for all teenagers should have a Facebook.

Juliana Boateng
Hi my name is Juliana Boateng and this is the first time that I am writing a book with fellow classmates. I am a senior now and just can' t wait to graduate. I am a fun, outgoing person and I hope that you have been able to see that through this book. Hope that you enjoy this and that it makes some type of difference in your life. Bye. CLASS OF 2008!!! WE'RE OUT HOLLA!!!!!!!

# Supporters

Nana Kwame Achampong
Aida Albarracin
Chris Albarracin
Mavis Amoakohene
Andarn Electro Services Corp.
Robert A. Barbera
Richard & Bettie Barnett
Sue Barsnica
Basheer, Olu, & Adi
Agnes Boateng
Emmanuel Boateng
Barbara Bohmer
Anita Buile
The Burns Clan
Nathaniel Butler Jr: Passaic County Prosecutor Office
Diane C. Buttel
The Cannons
Melissa Caparruva
Carrie & Nathan Butler
Good Luck- Mr. Castaneda
Estelita, Alejo, & Luvimin Catabay
Mrs. Cato
Joseph & Carmela Chirico
M. Karen Davis
Maureen Dreher
Robbie Beth Drossner MD
David Emma
Abiola Emmanuel
Ommotola Emmanuel
Don Erdman- Buy Our CD! Rescue Me
Faosat, Olu, & Adi
Wendy Faulk
Gale Feingold
Mr. & Mrs. Franklin
The Glenns
Dorothy Graves & Family
The Gyan Family
Miss Harpaul
The Hopkins Family
Demetrius Jeter
Dr. John Kronis
Lablessed1travel.com
Khiet Le

The Lewises
Lopina Family
Loretta
Mrs. Loyd
Lugo Family
Jason Mauriello
The Moseleys
Angela Nascondiglio
Anthony Nascondiglio
Dorothy Nascondiglio
Lisa Nascondiglio
Rocky Nascondiglio
Salvatore Nascondiglio
Thomas Nascondiglio
Ms. Loretta Okeke
Kevin Paiva
Joseph Ernso Pamphil
Pearl Street I Mgmt., LLC
Perez Family
Laverne Phillips
Joel L. Philistin
Mercedes Quinones
Miss O. Rodriguez
Rosel Family
RTA Travel Biz
Amy Samson
Ariel, Alexita, & Leanna Samson
Nick, Cheryl, & Angelina Samson
Donna Schimmenti
Kathy Schultz
Ms. Jaclyn Scotto
Aastha Shah
The Siaw Family
Dr. Laura C. Sottile Short Hills Chiropractic
The Thomases
Mr. Ray Toman
Rakesh Upadhyay
Vernell, Nate, & Jeremy
The Virgil Family: Donald, Natasha, & Devon
Sandra Yerike